Praise for **The Leader'**
to Influence

'Organizations across the globe are departing from traditional "command & control" leadership cultures in favor of more collaborative cultures where the ability to influence and gain followership is a vital skill. This book is an excellent resource for the manager who wishes to leverage their relationships for maximum impact.'

Dr. Robert Kovach, Director, Cisco Center for Collaborative Leadership

'In today's workplace technical knowledge alone is not enough to equip people for career success. Being able to build relationships with, and influence other people is the key. Clearly written and packed full of useful tools, examples and helpful tips by relationship experts Fiona Dent and Mike Brent, this invaluable book will help any manager understand how to make the most of their own style, build great relationships and learn how to influence other people more effectively.'

Linda Holbeche, Co-Director, The Holbeche Partnership and author of *HR Leadership* (2009) and *Aligning HR and Business Strategy* (2009)

'The higher you want to get in your career, the more important skillful influencing becomes. Mike Brent and Fiona Dent present clear, practical and detailed ways to deal effortlessly with difficult people and tricky situations elegantly and positively.'

Dr Mark McKergow, Centre for Solutions Focus at Work (www.sfwork.com)

The Leader's Guide to Influence

FT Prentice Hall
FINANCIAL TIMES

In an increasingly competitive world, we believe it's quality
of thinking that gives you the edge – an idea that opens
new doors, a technique that solves a problem, or an insight
that simply makes sense of it all. The more you know, the
smarter and faster you can go.

That's why we work with the best minds in business and
finance to bring cutting-edge thinking and best learning
practice to a global market.

Under a range of leading imprints, including *Financial Times
Prentice Hall*, we create world-class print publications and
electronic products bringing our readers knowledge, skills
and understanding, which can be applied whether studying
or at work.

To find out more about Pearson Education publications, or
tell us about the books you'd like to find, you can visit us at
www.pearsoned.co.uk

PEARSON
Education

The Leader's Guide to Influence

How to use soft skills to get hard results

Mike Brent and Fiona Elsa Dent

Financial Times
Prentice Hall
is an imprint of

Harlow, England • London • New York • Boston • San Francisco • Toronto
Sydney • Tokyo • Singapore • Hong Kong • Seoul • Taipei • New Delhi
Cape Town • Madrid • Mexico City • Amsterdam • Munich • Paris • Milan

PEARSON EDUCATION LIMITED

Edinburgh Gate
Harlow CM20 2JE
Tel: +44 (0)1279 623623
Fax: +44 (0)1279 431059
Website: www.pearsoned.co.uk

First published in Great Britain in 2010

Pearson Education is not responsible for the content of third party
internet sites.

ISBN: 978-0-273-72986-0

British Library Cataloguing-in-Publication Data
A catalogue record for this book is available from the British Library

Library of Congress Cataloging-in-Publication Data
Brent, Mike.
    A leader's guide to influence : how to use soft skills to get hard results /
Mike Brent and Fiona Dent. -- 1st ed.
        p. cm.
    Includes bibliographical references.
    ISBN 978-0-273-72986-0 (pbk.)
    1. Leadership. 2. Influence (Psychology) 3. Communication in
management. 4. Interpersonal relations. I. Dent, Fiona Elsa. II. Title.
    HD57.7.B748 2010
    658.4'092-dc22   2010024159

10 9 8
15

Typeset in Melior LT Std Regular by 3
Printed and bound in Malaysia (CTP-PPSB)

Contents

Acknowledgements

We would like to thank all our colleagues and friends at Ashridge for their support while writing this book. In particular, we would like to express our appreciation to those people who actively contributed to the content, especially the many leaders and managers we work with and who have shared their stories with us. We'd like to thank Dr David Beech for his contribution to Chapter 21 on Influencing Approaches. Our thanks also to Brief Institute London for the exercise on p. 169. And the following people deserve a special mention: Mark McKergow, Jenny Clarke, Graeme Robinson, Steve Sergeant, Eleanor Crowe, Dr Vicki Culpin, Adrian McLean, Maribel Albisua, Adrian Moorhouse and the Graphics Team at Ashridge.

Finally, we'd like to thank our editors Liz Gooster and Chris Cudmore at Pearson Education for their support and guidance.

Introduction

Why YOU need to read this book!

Relationships are the bedrock of human existence. As humans we are the most social species after ants, termites and bees! We are social and political animals with both an independent and an interdependent sense of identity. We are our relationships and the quality of our lives is a function of our relationships.

> ## Relationships are the bedrock of human existence

In business, no matter what your role, a high proportion of your working day is spent relating to other people. As a leader and manager you need to focus as much, if not more, on influencing, communicating, creating and developing effective working relationships, as you do on the technical or functional aspect of your job. So, whatever you do, whatever your level, and in whatever organisation, relationships matter for your effectiveness, reputation and success. You simply cannot be an effective leader or manager if you cannot effectively relate to and influence others.

How do managers become managers? In fact how did you become a manager? Did you go to university or college and study management for three or four years, then take a role as a trainee manager with coaching and supervision from highly qualified and experienced managers who gave you the benefit of their experience in frequent one to one sessions? If you are like most managers, then probably not! More likely you trained in a specific profession like engineering or marketing or finance, then joined a company, worked hard and because you were very good at your job, received a promotion to a managerial position. Or, maybe you didn't have that much formal training at all, and just worked your way up through the company. You were bright, worked hard, and were competent, flexible and resourceful, so you got promoted to a manager's post.

Sound familiar? If so, you are like the majority of managers we meet on our training programmes and workshops that we run all over the world. They have become skilled in their particular function, worked hard, shown excellent competence and been promoted. The only problem is that many have had no, or very little training in what it means to be a manager or a leader of people. They are mostly skilled in specialised areas and although they may well have interest in and an aptitude for people management, they have not had the specific training which would help them develop into and become skilled in this new role.

One manager shared with us that he was 'really scared' when he first became a manager as he had had no training and was well out of his comfort zone. Added to this there was the expectation that because he had been excellent in his previous role, he would know exactly what to do in his new role. If you further add a corporate culture in which to ask for help is seen as a weakness, then you have a recipe for management disaster. As he put it; 'I was just left to get on with it!' Simple really, or perhaps not!

Let's be clear about this, most leaders and managers have to juggle task focus and expertise alongside the most important aspect of leadership and management, dealing with people. On the one hand there is a focus towards task, action and results, and on the other the human and often intangible aspect of people management.

As a leader or manager your relationships are not restricted to your direct reports and boss, but reach out to all the people you come into contact with on a regular basis. This means that you need to become skilled in creating, developing and sustaining effective relationships at work. And it's not just a one way process, both parties, leader and led, need to actively work on this.

You need to become skilled in creating effective relationships at work

An important part of that relationship is how you go about getting commitment and buy in from others to do the things that need to be done. This is a critical aspect of contemporary management and leadership. There has also been a general shift from leadership by command and control to leadership through commitment and engagement. So, in this new way of working, how do you secure agreement from others? How do you get them to buy in to a project? How do you persuade and convince others? Engaging with others and gaining commitment starts with the quality of the relationship which will undoubtedly affect your success as a leader or manager.

We have written this book for two reasons: firstly, to help managers and leaders, like you, better understand the intangible, but critical, aspects of managing your various relationships at work. These aspects are communication, engagement, trust, energy, respect and above all, influence – aspects without which there cannot be effective performance. The second reason is to help you to have the confidence to act on this understanding by giving you the necessary tools and techniques.

This book is based on our own real life experiences working with leaders and managers from many different organisations; big and small, privately owned and public sector, local and international. All of the examples are taken from real management situations and the ideas and suggestions we put forward are all tried and tested. Early on in the book we focus on helping you to understand the nature of relations and your approach to them. We then move onto offering a range of tools, tips and techniques for you to add to your toolkit. We have written this book as a practical guide for practising leaders and managers. As such you may wish to read it from beginning to end or, indeed, it is equally useful to dip in and out of when you need inspiration or guidance when dealing with relationship issues.

We hope you find this book helpful and of practical value for creating, developing and maintaining effective and influential working relationships.

Your relationships: get them right

I t is important to recognise that successful relationships are an active process which requires a good deal of effort. The circumstances of a relationship are constantly changing. Once relationships are made it is important to acknowledge that they are worth nurturing to ensure that they continue to flourish. The following four stages and processes: identification, preparation, planning and implementation, will help you to focus and organise your relationships in order to get the best from them.

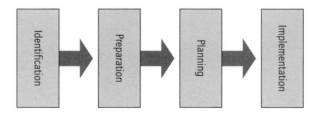

Constantly review and refine

Figure 1.1 The dynamic relationship model

1. Identification

Your relationship network is the full range of people you interact with during your working day. Begin by identifying and naming all the people who are in your relationship network. Having created the list of your relationships it is then important to assess the quality and importance of the relationships. One way of doing this is to evaluate each of your relationships on a scale of 1–10 with 1 being low quality or importance and 10 being high. Create your own version of the chart shown here to make your own list and score each person using the 1 to 10 scale for both quality and importance.

	MY RELATIONSHIP NETWORK – An example		
NAME	Quality of Relationship	Importance of Relationship	Development Notes
Jim	9	4	A good relationship continue as is
Bill	4	9	Needs work
Steffi	6	10	Needs work
Gerhard	8	5	Good relationship
Clare	2	8	Needs lots of work

Relationship Development

Creating the list and assessing the quality and importance of each of your relationships will help you to decide which are most important and require nurturing and development, and which are least important and so perhaps do not require so much investment.

2. Preparation

Understanding your relationship environment/ situation

Awareness and understanding of your environment and situation is vital to your success. Whatever the environment, from a large organisation to a small family unit, understanding and being aware of the behaviour and approaches that are acceptable and unacceptable is vital to your effectiveness.

> Awareness and understanding of your environment and situation is vital

In business these behaviours and approaches contribute to the culture of the organisation. So observe and be aware of:

▌ ways of working

   ▌ boss–subordinate relationships

   ▌ performance management processes

   ▌ interdepartmental relationships

   ▌ hierarchies vs. matrix

▌ written and unwritten rules

▌ what happens at meetings

▌ level of formality – how people dress, how people address each other (first names, etc.), the office environment (open plan or private offices) etc.

The culture of an organisation in this context can be defined as 'the way we do things around here'. Having a good understanding of the prevailing environment and the situation you are operating within is a good starting point for developing effective relationships.

FOR INSTANCE

Hugo is a corporate lawyer working in a large traditional law firm. Building relationships within his firm tends to be quite formal. Within the law firm everyone has their own office, hierarchies are observed and everyone dresses business smart! At work Hugo mirrors the typical professional businesslike approach. However, when he works with some clients he observes their environment is very different. The offices are very informal, all open plan, people wear jeans, meetings are organised informally and take place in open space and are often noisy and fun. The approach he uses with these people might be very different to the approach he uses with his colleagues. The key is to adapt, be flexible and select approaches, styles and skills that suit the environment and situation prevailing. If Hugo adopted his typical dress and behaviour with this client he may be seen as intimidating. So, when working with this client Hugo takes the opportunity to relax his formal dress and interacts more casually.

In addition to the general environment you operate in, you also have to take into account your own specific work situation and context. No two situations are the same as they involve:

▌ different people

▌ different attitudes

▌ different topics

▌ different moods

▌ different challenges.

When interacting with others it is easy to assume that just because you usually relate to someone in a particular way, this way will work under all circumstances. You must take into account that people react and respond differently depending upon the situation as well as the environment.

Focus on yourself

This means understanding yourself, your values and beliefs, your strengths and weaknesses, likes and dislikes, as well as your preferred approach when relating to others. Raising your level of self-awareness will help you enormously when deciding on the appropriate approaches and tactics to use when influencing and relating to others.

To raise your self awareness consider the following:

▎ your key strengths

▎ your weaknesses

▎ the things you like doing best

▎ the things you dislike doing most

▎ the things you most value

▎ your most important beliefs about the issue at hand

▎ the behaviours, skills and approaches you use most when influencing others.

We all develop habitual ways of operating, usually based on our strengths, skills, likes, values and beliefs. These habits become fixed behaviours which we use when interacting with others. These behaviours have consequences and again the important thing is to be aware of the behaviours you are using and the impact you are having on others. Sometimes it is appropriate to move out of your comfort zone and use behaviours that suit the situation and environment rather than those you use as a matter of habit.

Sometimes you'll need to use behaviours that suit the situation rather than those you use as a matter of habit

FOR INSTANCE

You might have a tendency to be forceful when relating to others, pushing your point of view expecting other people to join in the debate. However, this approach may not be appropriate in all situations and with all people. Becoming aware of your approach and your habitual behaviour patterns when interacting with others will help you to understand why some relationships are more successful and some more challenging or frustrating.

Focus on others

Understanding other people and reading them correctly is vital for effective relationship development. So the next stage in this process involves you looking at the other people involved. This means gathering as much information as possible about *all* the other people in your relationship network.

The things you should think about are:

▌ the job they do

▌ what seems to turn them 'on and off'

▌ how they communicate with you and others

  ▌ face to face and in writing

  ▌ talking/listening ratio

  ▌ body language used

  ▌ facial expressions used

  ▌ type of questions asked

  ▌ the balance of questions vs. statements

  ▌ what skills, approaches and techniques do they use when interacting and relating with you

▌ your feelings about them

▌ their interpersonal style.

FOR INSTANCE

One of the people in your relationship network is Clare. You have identified her as someone with whom you have a poor quality relationship. But as you rely on her for day to day support, it is nevertheless an important one, so you know you need to develop the quality of this relationship. You have been collecting information about Clare which may help you. For example, you notice she prefers to communicate by email, she is quiet, asks detailed questions and tends to keep herself to herself. You would define her style as introvert. You feel she is a little difficult to get to know.

These observations tell you that Clare isn't going to be easy to get to know, you will have to work hard to develop your relationship with her and clearly patience and flexing your style is going to be part of the process. You will need to draw her out in conversations and give her time to think and reflect about her perspective on issues so that she feels confident and comfortable in discussions. This means that you will have to adapt your normal style by slowing down your usual action oriented and extroverted approach.

By observing others and therefore raising your awareness about them you will be giving yourself a major advantage when interacting with them. There is a saying that 'information is power' and when used effectively information can help you to be more successful more frequently.

> By observing others you will be giving yourself a major advantage when interacting with them

Give yourself plenty of time to review before moving on to the next stages in the relationship process. You should spend some time analysing and reviewing your data so far. Ask yourself what all this information tells you about your environment and situation, the other people involved, and how this data can help you to develop effective and beneficial relationships. Begin to make a note of your thoughts and ideas for engaging and working with others.

3. Planning

What's your plan?

You should now be in a position to create a plan to develop the kind of relationship you want. This may involve a variety of different approaches for different people in different situations. For example, you may be building relationships with:

▌ your boss

▌ your boss's boss

▌ your work team

▌ external networks

▌ supplier/s

▌ customers/clients

▌ groups of colleagues.

You will find that there are many different ways of building relationships: formal, such as business meetings, presentations, development discussions; and informal such as, over lunch, managing by walking about, having a coffee and sending chatty emails. You may therefore decide on a combination of approaches, both formal and informal; whatever is appropriate for the people you are building relationships with. The real skill is to plan your relationship strategy, for example, by joining your professional body or local business enterprise group, and consider and plan your route when you 'walk about' so that you bump into the people you need to and want to.

4. Implementation

Approaches, style, skills and techniques to use

What works for one person or group may not work for others, and what works one to one may not work in a group meeting. The specific skills and approaches used will vary from situation to situation and person to person; the important point here is to realise that you must vary your behaviour, use different approaches and techniques to suit each different person, environment and situation.

Later chapters will explore a variety of techniques, approaches, styles and skills that will help you develop and manage your relationships with others to maximise your influence at work.

IN SUMMARY ...

Figure 1.2 summarises the relationship process.

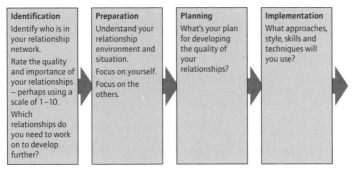

Identification	Preparation	Planning	Implementation
Identify who is in your relationship network.	Understand your relationship environment and situation.	What's your plan for developing the quality of your relationships?	What approaches, style, skills and techniques will you use?
Rate the quality and importance of your relationships – perhaps using a scale of 1–10.	Focus on yourself. Focus on the others.		
Which relationships do you need to work on to develop further?			

Constantly review and refine

Figure 1.2 The dynamic relationship process model

What's *your* relationship style?

A key factor in understanding and developing influential relationships is having an appreciation of your relationship style. Most of you have a preferred way of working with others. This is based on your habitual behaviour and comes about because you have found that certain approaches, behaviours and skills seem to work for you when interacting with others.

> ## Most of you have a preferred way of working with others

How would you describe your 'relationship style'? Do you tend more towards being outgoing or more reserved? Are you more people or task focussed? Do you worry about what people think or feel about you? How would you describe others' relationship style? What makes you describe them that way?

The relationship style questionnaire

Try the relationship style questionnaire (RSQ) shown here to identify your own preferred relationship style.

Look at the statements and words opposite and rank each

4		1		3		2	
I like to be of support to others		I am businesslike with others		I am enthusiastic with others		I express my opinions to others	
I like to be of support to others		I like to be businesslike with others		I am enthusiastic in my relations with others		I openly express my opinions to others	
I want to be friendly with others		I need time to get to know others		I like lively discussions		I like to be in control in relationships	
I tend to listen when with others		I tend to be more formal in relationships		I make relationships easily		I tend to focus on action in relationships	
I work towards co-operative relationships with others		I am reserved in initiating relationships with others		I have been described as high spirited by others		I am dominant in relationships with others	
My default position is to trust others		I am dependable in relationships		I get excited about the possibilities in relationships		I openly stand up for my own views	

	Harmony		Practical		Energetic		Powerful
	Collaborative		Realistic		Lively		Opinionated
	Open		Sensible		Active		Assertive
	Co-operative		Reasonable		Animated		Persuasive
	Supportive		Rational		Bubbly		Convincing
	Obliging		Equitable		Spirited		Compelling
	Accommodating		Level-headed		Passionate		Dominant
	Helpful		Logical		Cheerful		Competitive
	Caring		Consistent		Dynamic		Demanding
	Kind		Dependable		Vibrant		Challenging
	Total column 1		**Total column 2**		**Total column 3**		**Total column 4**

Relationship style questionnaire

row one to four with one being least like you and four being most like you. When answering the questions it is best if you think mainly about work-based relationships.

My preferred style (the highest score)   **Column** ___
Backup style (second highest score)   **Column** ___
My least preferred style (the lowest score)   **Column** ___

Figure 2.1 will help you understand and analyse your score. It shows the key to each of the styles, and summarises each style in turn.

No one style is best or worst, each style is simply different and each has its own positive and negative aspects. Your preferred style will have an effect upon the way you relate to others, how you are perceived by others and how others relate to you.

The relationship styles

Our approach is based on a two-dimensional model, where each of your preferences plays a role in the way you relate to people. The preferences are:

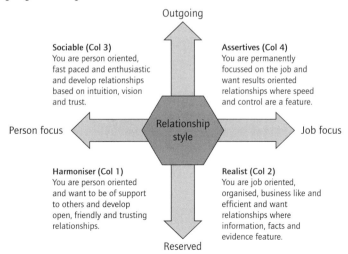

Figure 2.1 The relationship style model

▌ Are you more **outgoing** or more **reserved**?

▌ Are you more **person focussed** or more **job focussed**?

Your positioning on these preferences then translates into a relationship style which has been identified in the questionnaire.

▌ **Harmonisers** tend to be more reserved and person focussed. If you have a preference for this style you probably like to be supportive of others and develop open, friendly and trusting relationships with those people in your work-based relationship network. You see your role in relationship development at work as one that is tolerant of others and you are willing to work to collaborate for the sake of harmony. Sometimes you feel that other people take advantage of your good nature and expect too much from you. Others, usually those who have a different preference, may regard you as a people-pleaser who is constantly compromising for the sake of harmony.

▌ **Realists** tend to be more reserved and job focussed. If you have a preference for this style you want your relationships at work to be professional and businesslike and in service of the job at hand or your role in the organisation. You will tend to communicate in a matter of fact, organised and efficient way. You value information and facts and probably don't want people to get too personal or close to you. Some people may regard you as distant and formal perhaps even difficult to get to know. Certainly you will not readily share personal information unless it is appropriate to the situation and person you are communicating with.

▌ **Sociables** tend to be more outgoing and person focussed. If you have a preference for this style you energetically seek out opportunities to develop relationships at work. You are likely to have a wide range of different people in your network and you enjoy being with others and developing ideas and plans with them. You are extrovert, cheerful and friendly in nature. Sometimes you may be puzzled by other people's reaction to your natural vitality when they may regard you as rather intense and overly familiar. Others may also regard you as unpredictable and reckless.

▌ **Assertives** tend to be more outgoing and job focussed. If you have a preference for this style you are comfortable developing relationships at work especially when they are helping you to achieve your goals. In relationships you are comfortable presenting your point of view – even if it is unpopular and you tend to be regarded as someone who likes to be in control and speaks their mind. You prefer action oriented relationships and can appear to be rather insensitive and dismissive of others' feelings to some types.

Style characteristics

Each of the styles has positive and also potentially counter-productive characteristics (see table on p. 20). These characteristics often represent how people perceive each of the styles at its best and at its worst.

Once you have identified your preferred style you might also like to reflect on your ability to flex your style with different people. Successful leaders and managers recognise the importance of adapting and flexing their style to suit the people and situation.

> Successful leaders recognise the importance of adapting their style to suit the people and situation

Having identified your style preference, reflect on the following points, which will help you to understand more about the people in your relationship network. Turn to p. 6 and refer to the earlier Relationship network chart.

Relationship style			
Most Useful Characteristics		**Least Useful Characteristics**	
Sociable			
Inspiring	Energetic	Rebellious	Careless
Excitable	Passionate	Indifferent	Impetuous
Inventive	Persuasive	Volatile	Unconventional
Enthusiastic	High Spirited	Reckless	Irrational
Friendly	Perceptive	Slapdash	Intense
Assertive			
Self-assured	Determined	Aloof	Pushy
Challenging	Initiator	Insensitive	Serious
Opinionated	Persuasive	Domineering	Prejudiced
Directive	Action oriented	Unapproachable	Self-important
Forceful	Results oriented	Confrontational	Manipulative
Harmoniser			
Affable	Reciprocal	Wary	Vulnerable
Accommodating	Calm	Risk averse	Humble
Obliging	Caring	Compromiser	Needy
Amicable	Cheerful	Self Doubting	People-pleaser
Listener	Tolerant	Uncertain	Anxious
Realist			
Efficient	Factual	Formal	Distant
Orderly	Capable	Slow	Low energy
Conventional	Systematic	Unemotional	Critical
Sensible	Precise	Dispassionate	Nit picky
Meticulous	Structured	Moralistic	Judgemental

▌ Now rate the effectiveness of each of your relationships on a scale of 1 to 10 (1 being not effective and 10 being highly effective).

▌ Think about your work-based relationship network. Identify those relationships where you successfully use your preferred style and those where it seems not to work?

▌ Using a scale of 1 to 10 evaluate how appropriate your preferred style is for each of your current work-based relationships?

▌ What are the benefits of using your preferred style in your current relationships? Make a list of the benefits.

▌ What are the drawbacks/challenges of using your preferred style in your current relationships? Make a list.

▌ Apart from your preferred style, which other styles do you use with people? How comfortable/uncomfortable do you feel when using them? How successful are you when using them?

FOR INSTANCE

Akira is an MD of an international engineering company. He attended one of our workshops where we discussed the relationship style questionnaire. He found that his preferred relationship style is 'realist' and he told us that he tended to use this style with all his colleagues and had wondered why this worked well with some people but not with others.

He had a difficult relationship with his second in command – James – as he wanted to adopt a more friendly social approach where he chatted about non-work issues, which Akira saw as irrelevant and time wasting and became more and more frustrated.

Reflecting on this model, Akira realised that James tended towards a more sociable/harmonising style and therefore had different relationship needs to Akira. Following this realisation Akira adapted, and flexed his style to accommodate James's preference. This improved the relationship to such an extent that Akira and James now have a much more productive relationship.

Relating to others

The way you relate to others will affect the way others perceive you, how they treat you and how they react to you when you are interacting with them. For most of us, our preferred relationship style is our default approach. You tend to use this style because it has become habitual, easy to use and because it makes you feel comfortable.

While your preferred style will work for you much of the time, if you want to be a truly influential leader or manager it won't be the best approach all of the time. In order to get the best out of all your relationships it will, on occasions, be necessary to flex and adapt your style to ensure you reach truly effective outcomes and develop mutually beneficial and rewarding relationships.

When you know a relationship or situation isn't easy or comfortable, then it will be important to take some time to reflect on the people, their style and the situation. Then decide which style would be best to ensure that a good relationship developed and that you reach the outcome you desire. Just because you have to make use of a style which isn't your preferred style doesn't mean that you are changing your personality. It simply means that you are demonstrating your flexibility and adaptability to relate to others in a way that works for them and you.

Initially, flexing your style will involve conscious effort and is a critical skill for the influential leader or manager. However, as you become more adept at flexing your style you will find that you routinely weave the variations into your interactions with others and it becomes almost an unconscious process.

> Flexing your style will involve conscious effort

In a later chapter we will explore how you can develop self-awareness and understanding of others.

IN SUMMARY ...

You all have your own preferred way of relating to others. In order to get the best out of your relationships we believe you should:

- Identify your own preferences.
- Reflect on and understand how your behaviour impacts on others.
- Identify colleague's preferences as well as your own.
- Practise adapting and flexing your style to get the best from your relationships.

Understanding my relationships

I n our role as coaches and consultants we spend a lot of time talking to managers and business executives. When we speak to them we try to incorporate into our conversation two questions to help us understand more about work-based relationships.

▌ Why do people create relationships at work?

and

▌ What makes people maintain and develop relationships at work?

Leaders' responses to the questions have been fascinating and this chapter describes these responses and suggests ideas for making use of this data when engaging and influencing others. In this chapter there are several opportunities for you to work on some practical exercises and applications.

Why do people create relationships?

As you read this book you may like to think about why you create your own relationships. Consider those people you spend most time with at work, and ask yourself why you need or want that relationship? We discovered three main reasons why people start relationships, these are:

- **Work/functional reasons**. You may work with people because they could help you in your role or in the achievement of your goal. There may be a highly transactional element to the relationship, and if the work need were not there, you would not have a relationship with the person. Typically people you would relate to for work or other functional reasons could be:

  - people you work with on a regular basis
  - useful people in other functions
  - people you need to get the job done
  - experts
  - people who like networking.

- **Part of the work team**. In this area the common message that emerged from discussions with leaders and managers was that there was little choice in the relationship because:

  - it's a necessity – your boss/line manager
  - it's people you manage
  - it's your job description for a managerial role
  - your work is based in the department
  - you are thrown together in the work team.

- **Social/personal reasons**. The leaders and managers we speak to also suggest that work relationships could be for social reasons. They had established more of a personal relationship by having something in common, or by establishing a personal interest in each other. In this type of relationship there is a degree of choice. Reasons we've found for developing social and personal relationships at work could be with people who:

  - are supportive in their attitude

- you get on with
- have shared interests with you
- you have rapport with
- are in your community at work
- enjoy the social side of things
- you like
- are friends
- you need to establish personal contacts with
- you exchange robust views with
- help your thinking
- have something in common with you
- can be seen as helpful.

How to maintain and develop work relationships?

Making contacts and creating relationships is one thing, keeping them going is quite a separate issue. In order for any relationship to flourish it must be fed and nurtured, and for this to happen you have to devote time and energy to the process. So, think about what makes you spend your precious time developing and maintaining your relationships at work. People say things like *'instant rapport', 'we get on well', 'as a human being I want to interact with others',* and 'I like people'.

> In order for any relationship to flourish it must be fed and nurtured

So, it seems that personal or emotional attachment is of particular importance in establishing quality relationships that are mutually beneficial and rewarding. Typically the following reasons are mentioned by people when discussing their successful relationships:

- fun and social banter
- something in common
- to get things done
- new opportunities
- motivation
- provide a listening ear
- I like people
- getting where i want to go
- positive vibes
- like talking to them
- shared interest
- joint participation
- enjoyment
- having regular contact
- sharing knowledge and experience
- keeping people happy
- shared sense of humour.

When considering your own successful relationships think of which of the above apply to you and whether there are any others you could add.

People want one of two things from their work-based relationships; either a transactional relationship which focuses on work issues, or a work-based social relationship. Most people are not seeking to develop their work relationships into friendships outside the workplace. People do want friendliness at work but they don't necessarily want a deeper level of friendship.

The work-based relationship model

Effective leaders understand that it is important to reflect on the quality of all your relationships, and to use the information effectively. We have created the following model to help you do this. The model enables you to assess each relationship based on its value to you for work and for social reasons. Thinking about relationships in this context will help you to:

▌ Understand more about each relationship – why some are easy, difficult, challenging, frustrating, etc.

▌ Reflect about your motivations for each relationship

▌ Assess the value of each relationship to you personally and for business related reasons.

The features of each category are as follows:

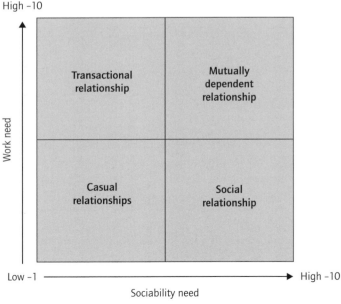

Figure 3.1 Work-based relationships model

Casual relationship – where there is a low work need and a low sociability need; a relationship that is not essential to core activities and is therefore a relationship that is peripheral and superficial. A relationship that is:

- non-essential
- with a person whom you have little contact with
- with a person you know very little about
- with a person for whom you have neutral feelings
- with someone you are aware of but don't have much contact with
- superficial.

FOR INSTANCE

Every morning when you arrive at the office you may say good morning and pass the time of day with the reception staff, perhaps chatting about their recent holiday or what they did at the weekend or previous evening. So, you are friendly to this person but they are low on both your work and sociability need scales – **a casual relationship**.

Social relationship – where there is a low work need and a high sociability need; where the main motivation for the relationship is an emotional connection which leads to friendliness. A relationship that is:

- non-essential for work reasons
- a person you choose to socialise with at work, perhaps having lunch with them
- a person you share ideas with and trust and respect
- a person who knows about you and you know about them at a more personal level
- a person you choose to spend time with.

FOR INSTANCE

Most of us have at least one person at work that we confide in, often this person isn't in our work group nor are they crucial to work, but rather someone with whom you have built a trusting relationship and whose opinions matter to you and whose company you enjoy – **a social relationship**.

▌ **Transactional relationship** – where there is high work need and low sociability need; those professional relationships necessary to get a job done. A relationship that is:

  ▌ essential for work

  ▌ with a person you would not naturally choose to spend time with other than for work reasons

  ▌ with someone you know little about but need to get the job done

  ▌ with someone you don't really feel strongly about

  ▌ with a person you know will be able to help you in your current role or project.

FOR INSTANCE

This is the person you know is crucial for getting your work done and someone you find difficult to relate to, so there is no other reason for the relationship to exist other than for job related reasons – **a transactional relationship**.

▌ **Mutually dependent relationship** – where there is high work need and high sociability need; where there is a balance of need from both a work and a social perspective. A relationship that is:

  ▌ based on mutual support and friendship

  ▌ with a person you know well and respect

  ▌ with someone you enjoy being with and is central to you getting the job done

▌ with someone who you enjoy sharing ideas, knowledge and experience with.

> ### FOR INSTANCE
>
> The person you know you want to have in your project team, you enjoy their company and you know they do a great job; possibly even more than this you make a good team – **a mutually dependent relationship**

Influential and relationally intelligent leaders recognise that they will have work-based relationships in all four categories; the important thing is to recognise which category each person falls into, and if it is appropriate for that particular person. If not, then you may have to invest some time and energy into developing the relationship further to ensure you are getting the best from it.

Using the work-based relationship model

We suggest you review all your work-based relationships using this model so that you begin to develop a greater awareness of the range of your relationships and the reasons why you have them.

You should ask yourself to what extent your relationships are based on work/functional need and to what extent they are a sociability need and then plot the various relationships on to the chart.

So for instance, let's say you have the following four people as part of your work-based relationship network:

▌ **Jenny** is a close friend, she is always empathetic, willing to listen and spend time with you. She works in a different department and you collaborate with her on a regular basis as she always adds value to any project she is involved with

▌ **Pete** is a quiet and industrious guy who works in the finance department and looks after all the accounts and budgets for your department, you'd be lost without him and while you are friendly towards him when you need something you don't know a lot about him other than he always gets the job done

▌ **Natalie** is a good mate, you often lunch together and go out after work and on occasions you've taken short breaks together; she's good fun and helps you relax

▌ **Lynda** is a fellow manager within the organisation, you often come across her in management meetings and pass the time of day with her but other than that have little to do with her.

Figure 3.2 is an example of how you can use this model.

High –10

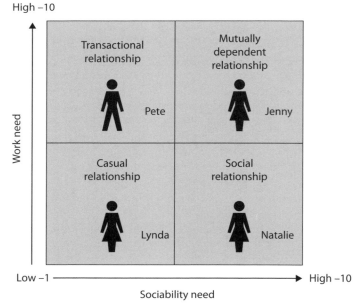

Figure 3.2 An example of the work-based relationship model

So, taking the four people in this model it shows the relationship with Pete is high work and low sociability, with Lynda it is low work and sociability, with Natalie it is mid work and sociability, and with Jenny it is mid work and high sociability. By applying this exercise to your own relationship network you will gain a better understanding of the dynamics of the network. You should then reflect about the implications and consequences of the way you interact and handle each of the people in your network. For example: you might be tempted to spend lots of time with Jenny as she is quite important on the work scale and you have a high level social relationship with her, yet Pete is possibly more important to focus on because of the higher work need. However you might not do that because you are not drawn to spend time with him.

Figure 3.3 summarises how you might perceive others based on the four categories:

Asking yourself about your reason for creating and maintaining a relationship will help you to identify your underlying motivations for relationships at work. This will lead to a greater awareness of your attitudes to relationship management and therefore a better understanding of your development needs in this area. This raised awareness will help you to understand:

▌ why you find some relationships easy

▌ why you find some relationships difficult

▌ why you find relationship development challenging

▌ how you might make adjustments to your current relationship development behaviour for greater effectiveness.

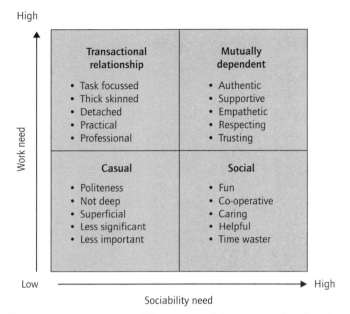

Figure 3.3 A summary of how one might be perceived and you may perceive others in each of the four work-based relationship categories

Practical work

In order to be able to apply this to your own work situation and analyse the dynamics of your relationships the following exercise will be useful. Using the data from your relationship network list (see p. 6) and using the blank work-based relationships model on p. 35, plot each member of your network onto the model.

Now analyse your model and reflect about what the pattern is telling you about your various work-based relationships by considering:

▌ the spread of relationships throughout the model

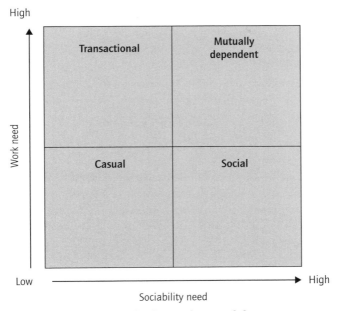

High

Work need

Low ——————————————————————→ High

Sociability need

Figure 3.4 A work-based relationship model

▌ the primary reason why you make relationships

▌ whether you like or dislike each person

▌ how important each person is to your effectiveness at work.

Typical relationship patterns include:

▌ **Mainly casual relationships**. Someone who is comfortable networking with others and collecting friends. For instance, people who invite you to join their social networking circle on one of the many web-based sites when you have only met them once. In other words a contacts collector. Could be regarded as friendly yet superficial.

▌ **Mainly transactional relationships**. A person who is businesslike, perhaps a political player, quite formal and someone you only see when needed for task related issues.

▌ **Mainly social relationships**. A chatty friendly person who takes an interest in people, what they are doing and likes to be in the hub of things. May appear to be disinterested in task issues as puts social interests first.

▌ **Mainly mutually dependent relationships**. Someone who is reliable, trustworthy, focussed, friendly and persuasive.

▌ **Mainly work-based relationships**. Someone who is driven by the job, not really interested in others except in service of getting the job done.

▌ **Mainly sociability-based relationships**. Someone who puts their need for social contact at work above their need to focus on the task. People and your relationship with them is all.

▌ **A good spread of relationship types**. Probably the ideal. Having people in all boxes is likely to be a reality for most of you.

Have a think about your own relationships, what patterns emerge and what are the implications for you.

> **Note down your thoughts and the implications for your relationship effectiveness:**

IN SUMMARY ...

This chapter, its content, model and exercises are a good starting point and will help you to reflect on and start to understand the dynamics of work-based relationships. Every relationship pattern will have its uniqueness so taking the time to do a personal analysis of your own work-based relationships is vital and will, of course, be where the main learning takes place. Later chapters will cover more about the features of good relationships and will introduce more tools and techniques to help you understand and develop your work-based relationships.

At this stage you should now:

- Be fully aware of the complete range of your work-based relationships.

- Understand more about your own motivations for creating and developing relationships.

- Continue to reflect about the categories of relationship and whether these are appropriate for your particular situation.

- Have some ideas about which relationships you need to invest more in, which you need to develop further and maybe which you could spend less time on.

What makes relationships go wrong?

E
ffective leaders and managers recognise that influencing is essentially a relationship skill rather than a strategy or business skill. But, even effective leaders and managers have experienced relationships which have gone wrong, some irreparably and others that are simply not as effective or rewarding as they used to be.

Rachel and Simone had worked in the same organisation for over five years. They did not work in the same department; Rachel worked in HR and Simone in Operations. During the five-year period they worked together on a range of projects and had always had an effective and open work-based relationship. They often lunched together and on occasions socialised outside work. Simone applied for a promotion within her department and Rachel was one of the people on the selection panel and unfortunately Simone was unsuccessful.

Shortly after the appointment Rachel bumped into Simone and suggested they lunch together, Simone said she already had a lunch date and Rachel thought no more about it. However, at lunchtime Rachel noticed that Simone was lunching on her own. There were other similar incidents, nothing dramatic, Rachel just felt that Simone had cooled off towards her.

Rachel felt that she hadn't done anything to warrant this sort of reaction. Simone's view was that Rachel had let her down during the selection process for the promotion and she was finding it difficult to feel positive towards Rachel.

Their relationship was never the same, they were able to work together but there was never the same warm easiness about their relationship.

We have heard many stories like the one above about relationships derailing and we have found that these stories can be categorised into nine themes:

- feeling let down
- breakdown in trust
- loss of respect
- communication misunderstanding
- one-way relationship
- envy and jealousy
- arrogance
- judgemental
- stubborn obstinacy.

The effective leader is constantly on alert for changes in the quality of their relationships

The effective leader and manager constantly has their antennae on alert for changes in the quality of their relationships and if they sense something going wrong they actively work to repair things. Many managers lack awareness of these changes and of their potential for derailment. Once a relationship starts to go wrong things can very quickly spiral out of control and little things, which in the past had no effect, will all of a sudden become big issues that impact on the decreasing quality of the relationship. This can lead to relationship breakdown which could ultimately affect your credibility and reputation if allowed to continue unchanged.

Each of the themes identified can play a part in relationship derailment, sometimes on their own or, more often than not, a combination of themes working together to challenge the quality of the relationship. Influential leaders and managers are aware of these possibilities and are always on the lookout for changes in others' behaviour. This could indicate that their relationship is potentially in trouble.

Theme 1

Feeling let down

Many people talk about the feeling of being let down by others is a major reason for a relationship going wrong. This is a highly emotive area and what one person identifies as feeling let down may not apply to another.

> Being let down by others is a major reason for a relationship going wrong

Some of the reasons people have given us for feeling let down include the following:

- not following through on a promise
- delivering a project late
- constantly delivering shoddy work
- being caught out with untruths
- gossiping behind someone's back
- not supporting a colleague at a difficult meeting.

Your personality type and approach to relationship

management will have an effect upon what makes you feel let down by others. You might like to identify the behaviours and attitudes that cause you to feel let down. Then talk to others in your influencing and relationship network to identify what affects them adversely. Being aware of what makes you and others feel let down is essential for successful relationships to exist.

Theme 2

Breakdown in trust

Trust is a feeling or emotion which is difficult to define and impossible to learn through intellectual means. It develops over time and is based on your experience of working with and relating to someone. Relationships with a strong sense of trust also have a sense of strength, security and confidence. Being able to trust your colleagues enables you to reach a high level of co-operation, openness and honesty which leads to excellent performance. A breakdown in trust, for whatever reason, means negative emotions and can lead to a blame culture and suspicion both of which will affect outputs and performance. As trust is one of the key elements for successful influencing, when it is missing influencing becomes very difficult. (See Chapter 9.)

Theme 3

Loss of respect

Respect is a quality attributed to an individual and, like trust, is based on your experience of that individual (for more on trust, see Chapter 9). Respecting another person is often related to your initial perception of them and your subsequent experience in your relations with them. For instance, the respect you have for another person may be based on their expertise in an area. If this expertise is challenged and you discover they are not quite as 'expert' as they would have others believe, then this may have an effect upon your level of respect. When you are involved in an influencing discussion, the presence of mutual respect will undoubtedly help the process move more efficiently. If one person lacks respect for the other then distrust and suspicion about the other person's motives will be present. This can also negatively affect the way that you work together.

Theme 4

Communication misunderstanding

This can be caused by many things including use of language, lack of clarity, ambiguity, difference of style and personality differences.

FOR INSTANCE

One of your team has been working hard to deliver a project to you early so that you have plenty of time to absorb it before incorporating it into a larger paper for presentation to your senior board. You thank the team member and tell them they've done a pretty good job. Later on in the day you overhear the same team member having a moan to a colleague that you didn't appreciate their efforts and seemed to take all the hard work for granted and all you said was that they'd done a 'pretty good job'.

From your perspective, you know your colleague did go the extra mile and had hoped that they realised this and on reflection perhaps you didn't take sufficient time to indicate your appreciation sufficiently well.

In this case you are lucky that you overheard the conversation as you can now repair any damage done quickly by showing your team member how their work has contributed to the bigger project and how important it is to its success.

Misunderstandings like this are difficult to avoid – the important issue is to remedy them speedily.

Other important aspects of misunderstanding are where people have different personality types or cultural backgrounds, and therefore express themselves very differently. There are a number of personality questionnaires which can help you to understand differences. For example, you may have come across the Myers Briggs Type Indicator (MBTI). This personality questionnaire identifies your preferences in four different areas and we want to focus on one of these areas, which relates to how you make decisions. Typically, you will have a preference for one or the other of either *thinking orientation*, where your decisions are based on objectivity, justice, policy and facts, and you tend to be regarded as logical, detached and analytical; or *feeling oriented* where your decisions are more subjective and based on interpersonal involvement and you are regarded as harmonious, collaborative and tender-hearted. These differences are often a recipe for misunderstanding as both types of preference process decisions differently and this can lead to massive misunderstanding even when they are in agreement about the outcome. In situations like this, it is important to be aware of these processing differences and develop your own strategies to deal with these differences. This, of course, is easier when you are well known to a person and understand their communication style; the golden rule here is to avoid misunderstanding by constantly clarifying, testing understanding and summarising to ensure you are both on the same track.

Theme 5

One-way relationship

When one party feels they put more effort into the relationship than the other. Usually, this is a feeling that develops over time and often manifests itself by a feeling of being let down by another due to lack of support or reciprocity.

FOR INSTANCE

Janice, who was an IT Consultant, told us about a colleague she had worked with for several years – Sean – who consistently took advantage of her good nature to help finish off projects and provide support when things got too pressurised. Sean was not a particularly organised person and often agreed to take on projects without thinking about his current workload. When this happened, the deadline approached and it was clear that without some help the project would be unfinished. Janice, on the other hand, was a well organised and efficient project manager and often offered to give Sean a hand to get things finished. This pattern of behaviour continued on and off for several years, and it was only when Janice needed a bit of support one afternoon to get one of her projects completed for a very tight deadline, that she became aware of the one sided nature of their relationship. Sean was not very busy himself, but when Janice asked him for some help he wished he could, but he had to leave on time to meet a mate for a drink. Janice was upset by this rebuff and reflected that this actually wasn't the first time this had happened over the years – the realisation suddenly hit her that Sean was taking advantage of her good nature to support him, but wasn't reciprocating by being there when she needed him.

Influential leaders understand the importance of reciprocity

Influential leaders and managers understand the importance of reciprocity in relationships and the need to support and be there for colleagues. One element of good influencing depends upon good quality relationships. These must develop over time and are often based on mutual support and reciprocity.

The following four derailment themes relate to personality

traits that many people find difficult to deal with. These traits are arrogance, envy, judgemental behaviour and stubborn obstinacy.

Theme 6

Arrogance

This has a hugely negative impact and when people begin to display this trait it can lead to speedy relationship derailment. Arrogant people are generally unaware of the impact they are having and often lack any genuine interest in others. They also exhibit an unwarranted degree of self-importance demonstrated by the overuse of the words 'I' and 'me' in conversation, by constant self-reference and boasting about their own achievements, by name dropping to show how important they are and by generally demonstrating a disdain for others.

Theme 7

Envy and jealousy

These occur when one person in a relationship begins to feel envious of another and this envy turns into jealousy, which in turn has an effect on the way the person interacts with you. Often it is displayed by subtle changes in behaviour towards you; little digs, references to 'how lucky you are', spending less time in your company, gossiping behind your back, non-verbal changes such as difficulty in maintaining eye contact. There are, of course, many reasons for someone beginning to feel jealous or envious. Some of those suggested to us by leaders and managers include:

▌ being promoted out of a team to be the team leader

▌ being promoted to a more senior position

▌ developing new relationships with a different group of people

▌ others getting jobs you feel you are better qualified for or that you deserve more

▌ finding out that someone doing the same job as you gets paid more

▌ perceiving that others get better perks than you do.

Envy and jealousy are difficult to detect and challenging to deal with, especially if this is a feature of someone's personality. Influential leaders and managers realise that the best way of dealing with this is to work hard at the relationship and continue to demonstrate that these people are valued members of your network.

> Envy and jealousy are difficult to detect and challenging to deal with

Theme 8

Judgemental

We all judge others to some extent. We make judgements about others based on their appearance, behaviour, language, job, qualifications and many other attributes. When we talk about judgemental, we mean those people who have strong opinions and views about every subject, whether they really know about it or not and liberally share their opinions with others. Usually this type of person is a 'time eater' as they not only share their views but also explain them in detail. Allied to this is their inability to listen to and understand your views and this is what makes them so difficult. When a person constantly displays judgemental behaviour, it really challenges your patience and makes it very difficult to influence them. Try 'googling' judgemental people, there are over 1 million results. We didn't look at all 1 million but the first few were very definitely highly critical of judgemental people and how difficult they are to work with. The easy way out is to walk away from them and ignore them, but this is not always possible. What if the person is your boss, or a senior colleague? The influential leader and manager will develop coping strategies, often involving behavioural adaptation on their own part, to deal with people like this. For example, you could try the following:

- use assertive and rational influencing approaches more than you would typically.

- if interrupted by a judgemental person (often one of their traits) then quickly state something like – 'if you'd just let me finish' or 'before you interrupted I was going to go on to explain …'.

- recognise that with judgemental people the best you can hope for is their acceptance of, rather than real commitment to, your ideas.

Theme 9

Stubborn obstinacy

This personality trait often defines people who are extremely self-contained and change resistant. They are therefore difficult to develop relationships with and to influence in any way. People with this tendency will often be regarded as 'anti-social', independent, isolationist and inflexible. The influential leader and manager will recognise that everyone is different and while this type of person is a challenge, their behaviour is often borne out of fear. While they may not be at the centre of your influencing and relationship network, you will undoubtedly come across people like this and have to deal with them. Patience is the answer here, supported by determined questioning to understand their perspective and to show them that you care. This can then be followed by your skilful use of some of the techniques explained in this book, for example, reframing, linking and building, and using appreciative techniques to sow seeds of interest in the other person's mind and to begin to get them to work with you.

IN SUMMARY ...

All of these relationship derailers are avoidable. The key here is to be aware of the subtle changes in both your own and others' behaviour that can inadvertently lead to relationships going off track. As an influential leader and manager you should:

- Look out for cues and clues that might indicate changes in a person's attitude towards you which might lead to derailment of the relationship.

- Be willing to adapt and adjust your own behaviour to accommodate difference.

- Develop coping strategies for the different types of people you encounter on a day-to-day basis.

- Ask for and give feedback to others so that your relationships are open, trusting and respectful.

- Ask questions to clarify when you feel things may be going wrong.

- Don't get involved with gossip – be straight and open with others.

- Learn from your mistakes.

- Model and learn from others.

5

Relationship networking

I n recent years the concept of social networking has become very popular, not only physically networking with people but also virtual networking via the huge number of 'social networking' websites that exist today (Facebook, MySpace, Linkedin, Friends Reunited, to name a few). For many people networking is simply about numbers and having loads of contacts.

Influential leaders and managers recognise that what is important is the quality and not the quantity of people in their network. Having a range of open networks in your work setting will help you to avoid isolation and insularity. It will enable you to develop a broad range of relationships across the organisation, so that you have multiple access points for information sharing and gathering, both of which are invaluable when influencing and working with others.

> Influential leaders recognise that what is important is the quality and not the quantity of people in their network

However, networking isn't simply about collecting people's names, telephone numbers and email addresses. It's about investing time and energy to develop and nurture relationships so that both parties can get the best out of the relationship. Understanding and using the appropriate skills and behaviours (discussed in this book) in each of your relationships will help you to build high quality relationships, which will undoubtedly contribute to your influencing success and ultimately your performance at work.

Let's face it, you might know hundreds of people, but knowing them is one thing. Being able to rely on them and trust them is quite another. The first step in networking is to be aware of the people in your various relationship networks, work life, social life and family life are typically the three most important networks in any of our lives. Of course each of these networks can be subdivided and the first stage of understanding is to create a network map.

The six step process

Here's a six step process for mapping your relationships, which will help you to analyse and review the quality, process and benefits of the people you interact with on a regular basis.

Step 1

Get a blank sheet of paper and some coloured pens. We find that an A3 sheet is best, A4 is usually too small, but will do if nothing else is available.

Step 2

Decide which group of people you wish to focus on – work/ family/social.

Step 3

This is the fun bit, create a network map by placing yourself in the centre and then adding all the people you interact with around that central core where the primary relationship is linked directly and secondary relationships are linked to their primary relationship (for instance: a colleague you work with may be a departmental manager and you may have a relationship with some of his/her team so the primary relationship would be with your colleague with secondary relationships with the team.) Figure 5.1 is an example of a very basic network map.

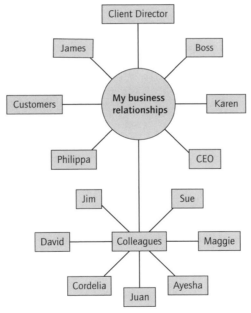

Figure 5.1 Relationship Network Map – 1

You should expect your own to be rather more complex, showing all your relationships and the interconnections between them.

Step 4

You are now in a position to review and analyse your network map to help you better understand the basis and quality of each of your relationships. In order to help you with this analysis and review, we find it useful to annotate the map with helpful comments about the quality of your relationship with each person (see Figure 5.2 below for an example). For instance, identify those people who are:

▐ most and least useful to you

▐ best and least known to you

▐ liked and disliked by you

▐ in successful or problematic relationships with you

▐ worthy of more/less effort to develop your relationship.

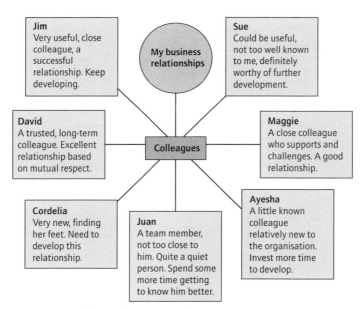

Figure 5.2 Relationship Network Map – 2

Step 5

You now have a full picture of your current relationship network including an analysis of the quality of each relationship. The next step is to develop your action plan.

Step 6

Examine your map and note down ideas for making best use of existing relationships and identify other people you wish to develop relationships with.

IN SUMMARY ...

Here are some tips from successful networkers:

- Develop connections at all levels in the organisation:
  - senior people provide you with connections which can help you to understand broader contexts and support you when influencing
  - lateral connections ensure you relate to people with similar organisational challenges to yourself and also provide you with brainstorming buddies
  - people junior to you in the organisation help with your managerial and leadership reputation, and will help you to be seen as a good coach. This will also provide you with early warning of talent for development.
- Develop relationships with experts and other contacts outside your organisation to help provide relationships for getting a different perspective, innovative working and potential future opportunities.
- Make a conscious effort to notice what works and what doesn't in terms of your behaviour for each person in your relationship network. Then vary your behaviour and technique to suit the situation and person you are interacting with.

- Where possible try to connect with people at both a work and personal level, getting the balance right can pay significant dividends.

- Remember networking is a two way process. It is important to recognise that you both contribute to and get sufficient from each relationship by being committed to more than your own self interest. So:

  - in conversations engage fully with others

  - focus on drawing others into conversations and listening to and developing their ideas as well as sharing your own

  - when disagreeing focus on the issue at hand not on the person

  - follow through on your commitments to ensure your reputation remains intact and grows.

6 Creating the right impression

Do you ever think about the impact you have on someone when you meet them for the first time? Do you reflect about the longer lasting impression you have on others when you interact with them? Do you care?

When it comes to relationship management these are important questions. If you don't think about it and even worse if you don't care, then it is likely that you will have problems when interacting or relating to others. Any lack of knowledge, understanding and awareness in relation to impact and impression management will affect your ability to build and develop effective relationships.

What is impression management?

Quite simply it is the effect you have on others and the feelings you leave them with when you have been interacting with them in any situation. Getting it right is about ensuring you give yourself the best possible

Becoming more aware of the image you are portraying is a key element opportunity to create a positive and lasting impression. Becoming more aware of the image you are portraying to others is a key element of impression management. So, like it or not, impression is based on the initial impact you make and then the subsequent feeling that you leave others with each time you interact with them. Image and impression management are vital in both creating and maintaining effective relationships.

The importance of impression management is highlighted by Michael Shea in his book *Personal Impact*.

> When we see someone for the first time, the initial sound/visual 'bite' – a combination of their looks, their dress, their bearing and the tenor of their opening remarks – become deeply etched in our minds and affect our attitudes to them!

When you meet someone for the first time, or enter into a dialogue with a person you don't know very well, you typically ask yourself a range of questions:

▌ What do I think/feel about this person?

▌ Do I like this person?

▌ Can I work with this person?

▌ Do I trust this person?

▌ Do I respect this person?

▌ Do I care what this person thinks about me?

This isn't necessarily a conscious process; you ask yourself these questions in your mind in order to assess your views about another person to determine how you will react to them, and whether or not you wish to develop a relationship with them.

The implications are that each and every one of you must be aware and take care to create and develop a positive impression on others. Remember your reputation is created by other people's impression of you. Creating and developing the right impression is one of the first opportunities you have to begin a relationship with another person. Get this right and you are off to a flying start, misjudge and get it wrong and you will have much work to do to get it back on track.

> **FOR INSTANCE**
>
> ## Getting it wrong
>
> Terry was a successful senior systems analyst working for a large UK corporation as team leader of a small team developing online material for their website. He'd been in the job for four years and was efficient, effective and creative. His boss had indicated that perhaps he should think about going for a more senior management position.
>
> He didn't have to wait long and as expected got an interview. The panel included his own line manager, his boss and an HR Manager. Everyone on the panel knew Terry except the HR manager. Terry thought the interview went well and was surprised when he didn't get the job. He just didn't know what went wrong; his boss told him he simply didn't create the right impression at the interview.
>
> So what did he get wrong? Simple really, he didn't make enough of an effort with his appearance and manner during the all important interview, and this was interpreted as lack of interest/ commitment to the promotion. There was nothing really dramatic, but Terry had not put in any effort to 'brush up' or to prepare for the actual interview and gave an overly casual impression.
>
> ## Getting it right
>
> In any selection interview, whether it's with your current employer or with a new organisation it is important to not only know your stuff about the organisation and the job but also to show the interview panel that you are a serious contender by getting your overall appearance correct. So:

■ Wear smart and appropriate clothes.

■ Pay attention to overall appearance, making sure it's appropriate.

■ Think about how you will introduce yourself, offer to shake hands and have a good opening line prepared – For example 'Hi, my name is . . ., I'm really looking forward to understanding more about your organisation and the role.'

■ Think about, plan and rehearse the key messages you want to get across. Anticipate some of the questions they might ask and prepare your responses in advance.

■ The more work you do to prepare for any selection interview, the better impression you will create; in general interviewers like people who are obviously well prepared as this indicates real interest in the role.

■ Don't be over familiar, even if you know them.

Impression management is not simply about first impressions, it is about those lasting impressions you make on others

For good relationships to exist impression management is not simply about first or early impressions, it is about those lasting impressions you make on others. What you need to do is to ensure that these impressions are as positive as possible. This means that every time you interact with someone you leave them with an impression of yourself which is used to inform all future interactions.

The first things you notice when interacting with someone are:

Visual impression – which is based on the things you notice about the person and the details and specifics you become aware of, observe and take in. This is based on, for example:

▮ clothes

▌ grooming

▌ the way you carry yourself

▌ facial expression.

This then leaves you with thoughts, feelings and reactions to the person which lead to you forming either a positive or negative impression of the person.

FOR INSTANCE

You are chairing a meeting with some clients; you have arrived early and are already in the room setting things up. The clients begin to arrive and you are ready to greet and acknowledge them but as they walk in they systematically ignore you, continue their conversations and don't offer a handshake or a good morning. How do you feel? What opinion are you now forming of these clients?

This happened to a consultant friend of ours recently. This left him wondering why he had been invited to run the meeting and furthermore left him with an extremely negative perception of the participants. This also negatively affected the process and outcome of the meeting.

Of course the consultant could have taken the initiative and approached them discretely and introduced himself and welcomed them to the meeting.

For a better impression to be created by the clients – all they had to do was simply greet the consultant, shake hands and introduce themselves and things would have been more positive.

Body language – is the rich combination of body posture, gestures, facial expression and eye contact. It is also how you as an individual express these when interacting with others.

Vocal usage – the way you use your voice – accent, pace, tone, pause, pitch, rhythm and emphasis and its effect on others.

Language – the words you use have to be clear, appropriate, direct, descriptive and relevant.

How you use your body language, vocal usage and language when interacting and engaging with others can either support or negate the message you are trying to convey. In particular it is important to convey congruence between all three by matching to ensure your language, body language and vocal usage are all in tune and conveying the same message. (There are many other books written which go into tremendous detail on this topic – e.g. Pease.)

This leads to **An Impact Being Made** which is the first impression you leave people with and may lead to **Rapport Being Developed.** This encourages **Interest to be Generated** which can lead to **Liking being Generated** (see Figure 6.1 below).

Figure 6.1

Taken together these aspects of your behaviour are the major components of impression management. Impression is important because it contributes to your overall relational credibility and reputation. So, the next time you are talking to one of your colleagues, imagine you are meeting them for the first time. What would you notice and what impression would that leave you with?

Focus on 'Brand You'

One way of focussing on the impression you create is to think about yourself as a brand. Tom Peters was probably the first management guru to suggest the idea of creating and promoting yourself as a brand. By applying the same principles to 'Brand Me' as marketers apply to their products, you too can create a successful brand for yourself. By thinking about yourself as a brand you will really be focussing on your skills, strengths, ambitions, dreams and goals.

To develop your 'Brand Me' you should ask yourself questions in six different areas:

1 What do I stand for?

2 What are my ambitions?

3 What roles do I take in life?

4 Who am I?

5 What are my objectives in life?

6 How will I measure success?

The model below summarises this

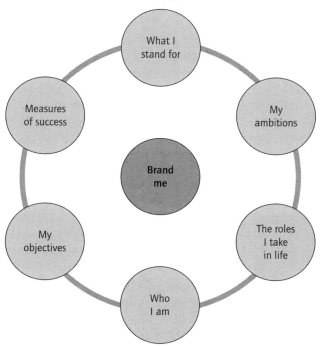

Figure 6.2

Here are some additional thoughts relating to the sort of questions you might like to consider under each of the headings.

1 What do I stand for?

▌ What are my personal values and beliefs that I hold dear?

▌ Using the list below select your top ten personal values – this is not an exhaustive list so add your own. This will help you to clarify what you stand for.

Ambitious	Adventurous	Authentic
Autonomous	Benevolent	Brave
Capable	Challenging	Change
Committment	Community	Competence
Co-operation	Creativity	Curiosity
Dedicated	Democracy	Decisiveness
Dependable	Determined	Egalitarian
Empathetic	Expert	Fair
Faithful	Family	Frank
Freedom	Fun	Goodwill
Harmony	Honesty	Honour
Imaginative	Independent	Innovative
Inspiring	Integrity	Justice
Knowledge	Leadership	Love
Loyalty	Money	Open
Original	Patriotic	Peace
Perfection	Pleasure	Power
Privacy	Prosperity	Punctuality
Radical	Reliability	Respect
Security	Self-respect	Self-sufficient
Sincere	Single-minded	Success
Teamwork	Tolerance	Tranquil
Trust	Truth	Unique
Variety	Wisdom	

2 **What are my ambitions?**

▌ What are your dreams?

▌ What do you hope to achieve in your life?

3 **What roles do I take in life?**

▌ Think about the different people in your relationship network and the roles you play in relation to them.

▌ Which roles are most/least important?

4 **Who am I?**

▌ What are my strengths and weaknesses?

▌ What do I enjoy doing?

▌ What do I dislike doing?

▌ What would I like to be doing?

▌ How might others describe me?

5 **What are my objectives in life?**

▌ What do I want to achieve in my life?

▌ What would I like to be remembered for?

6 **How will I measure success?**

▌ You could refer back to your values here.

▌ What does success mean to me?

Each of these questions is interlinked and answering one will undoubtedly help you answer some or all of the others. Having answered and analysed your responses to the six questions you should now be in a position to create a summary of your brand. Again, like any brand you should think about your personal story (for more on storytelling see Chapter 20), so the challenge is for you to express your brand as a short summary statement, a motto and a symbol that reflects your brand.

FOR INSTANCE

Brand Fiona

SUMMARY: The people in my life are my key focus, my family, my colleagues and my clients. My passion is to support and help them to be self-reliant, be the best they can be and achieve their own success. I can do this by:

- Keeping myself fit and healthy
- Demonstrating commitment and passion for my work
- Being there for others and helping them
- Developing new and creative approaches to people development
- Having fun, enjoying work and keeping a good balance in my life.

MOTTO: To be true to myself, authentic with others, seize the moment and live life to the full.

SYMBOL:

Like any commercial brand you will have to continually refine and develop the focus of your personal brand as you go through your life. Some aspects of your brand will remain stable – those areas affected by your closely held values and beliefs, however, others will change as you mature, develop and experience life. Having a personal brand gives you a focus and structure for your impression management, and provides you with an elevator pitch when interacting with others. An elevator pitch is a concise and clear summary of your point of view on any given topic. Imagine you are in a lift/elevator with a client and you only have 2 minutes to get your point across, what do you say?

FOR INSTANCE

You start a new job and during the first few days you are meeting lots of different people most of whom say something like tell me a bit about yourself. Having spent some time reflecting about values, ambitions, roles and objectives you should be able to communicate in a positive and succinct way a clear impression of yourself. Such as, saying a little about why you are joining the company, what you are looking forward to, your previous experience and a little personal information.

IN SUMMARY ...

Creating and managing the impression you make on others is key to your success as a leader and manager. Every time you interact with someone you are having an impression upon them. This impression will then have an effect upon the way they deal with you in the future. So:

- Think about the impression you want to make in any given situation.

- Analyse the context and environment.

- Plan.

- Dress and act appropriately.

- Constantly be aware of others by gauging and reading their reactions to you in different situations.

Listening

7

istening is a complex process. In our view people who have mastered the art of attentive listening do two key things:

▌ ask frequent and appropriate questions

▌ use their eyes as well as their ears to observe and notice the other people they are communicating with.

The influential leader and manager recognises the importance of attentive listening as one of their key tools for success. In our experience, many of the leaders and managers we work with indicate that they find it difficult to listen effectively, and they believe others do not listen to them. In fact, research has shown that most of us listen at less than 30 per cent efficiency. Listening is the most used of the communication skills yet unlike speaking, reading and writing no one teaches us how to do it. Influential leaders and managers understand the importance of this skill, and their ability to demonstrate

Attentive listening is one of the key tools for success

this to others. They therefore work hard to develop their listening skills.

There are two other important aspects for effective listening.

▌ listening to hear what is being said, both the words and the non-verbal communication that supports the words

▌ listening to understand what has been said, this involves testing understanding, clarifying and summarising as well as asking questions.

So, when in dialogue with another person you will be watching them, hearing them and working to understand them. It's not just about hearing the words; the really skilful listener grasps the facts, feelings and emotions behind the words. When you are listening it is very easy to become distracted and this can undermine your listening capability. Some of the major distractions to be aware of include:

▌ Physical and environmental distractions

   ▌ external noise, for instance, phones ringing, traffic noise, laughter and playing with mobile phones

   ▌ doodling, finger tapping, shuffling papers and playing with pens

   ▌ room temperature – too hot or too cold.

▌ Your own internal distractions

   ▌ your reactions to the speaker, caused by dislike, lack of respect or trust

   ▌ your reactions to the topic, disinterest, disagreement, heard it all before, or prejudice

   ▌ your frame of mind, you may have some other pressing matter on your mind which is affecting your listening behaviour

   ▌ premature judgement

   ▌ planning and rehearsing your response.

▌ Distractions caused by the speaker

▌ mannerisms

▌ appearance or dress

▌ vocal tone, pace or accent

▌ language used, too simple or too complex, jargon, technical, dialect.

Poor listeners are easily distracted and don't understand the importance of listening with both their ears and their eyes. As well as being easily distracted, poor listeners are also too keen to speak themselves and interrupt others so that they can put their point of view across. It's really all about your attitude as well as skill. You will learn more by adopting a positive attitude when listening to others. You will learn something new about the topic, the speaker's views or about the speaker themselves.

Poor listeners don't understand the importance of using their ears and eyes

Good listening behaviour involves using a combination of:

▌ preparing to listen by opening your mind and concentrating on the speaker/s

▌ putting the speaker at ease and building a rapport by demonstrating attentiveness and interest through your body language, facing the speaker, eye contact (but not constant), posture, slight head movements, nodding, smiling and other empathetic utterances, (mm ..., yep, etc.) and above all avoid fidgeting

▌ maintaining an open mind and not jumping to conclusions

▌ recognising key words and themes, not just facts or emotions

▌ listening to tone and volume to help you understand the speaker's thoughts and views

▌ testing understanding and clarifying by asking appropriate questions

▌ summarising in your own words what you believe you have heard

▌ picking up on clues and cues to hear what's not being said and then clarifying to ensure you have interpreted correctly

▌ avoiding interrupting.

Above all, remember that a well timed and appropriate question will demonstrate your listening skill to others.

Self-assessment quiz

Why not try this short quiz to assess your current skill level.

Look at the questions below and rate yourself using this 5-point scale.

Now assess your skill level, how many questions did you answer with 'often or always', these are your listening strengths. The others are all areas for improvement.

In an influencing and relationship development context, listening is paramount to your success. In order to influence and relate to others effectively you have to be able to express your thoughts, ideas and point of view and also to take account of and understand others' thoughts, ideas and points of view. Influential managers recognise that influencing is not about 'getting your own way'. Rather, it's about working together building relationships in order to reach effective outcomes which all parties can buy into. In order for this to happen you have to listen to and work with others.

		Never	Sometimes	Usually	Often	Always
1	I like to listen to others talk					
2	I encourage others to talk to me					
3	I listen to people even if I don't like them					
4	I look at others when listening to them					
5	I use encouraging gestures and noises when listening					
6	I let people finish what they are saying					
7	I tend to re-state what someone has said to test understanding					
8	I question others to ensure full understanding					
9	I watch out for non-verbal clues when listening					
10	I listen for ideas and concepts as well as facts and information					

FOR INSTANCE

Fabio was a consultant who was puzzled by his lack of ability to win new business. He was successful in all other aspects of his job, but this one important area eluded him. This was holding him back and he wanted to understand what he was doing wrong. He asked Mike to sit in on his next sales meeting to provide him with feedback.

Mike noticed very early on in the meeting some of Fabio's main problems. He had a tendency to transmit lots of information, to talk at the people, he didn't ask them many questions at all and didn't notice the cues the clients were giving him. It was clear to Mike that Fabio had not 'heard' what the client wanted as he had not explored their needs and the few questions he did ask were closed.

Mike's feedback to Fabio was that if he'd been the client he would have felt ignored as he hadn't listened and taken onboard any of their ideas or needs.

IN SUMMARY ...

Skilled listeners:

- Pay attention.
- Indicate their interest.
- Listen without prejudice or judgement.
- Observe and notice others' body language and vocal usage.
- Ask questions to expand the other person's thinking.

and as Ernest Hemmingway said:

> I like to listen. I have learned a great deal from listening carefully. Most people never listen.

Quality questioning

Asking a question is one of the key components of the influential relationship manager's toolkit. Like listening, the skill of questioning is not one we are taught at school, it's something you learn for yourself. Really successful relationship builders and influencers understand the importance and value of the well timed, well structured and appropriate question. When you are trying to build a relationship and influence people they like their ideas and perspectives to be sought and heard. Too many of us share our thoughts and ideas, and then never really listen to or understand where the other parties are coming from.

> Successful relationship builders understand the importance of the well timed, well structured and appropriate question

First, you need to understand the importance of questions for successful influencing. They:

▌ ascertain facts and positions

▌ indicate interest in others and thus get their buy in

▌ help you get useful information to share and build on

- involve others and enable them to offer their views and perspectives on an issue

- enable you to probe for the other parties' true feelings and thoughts

- empower the questioner through the information gathered during the process

- help you to assess how best to progress when influencing.

Understanding why you use questions when influencing is important. Many people think that good influencing is only about having a good point of view and being able to argue your point effectively. Our experience tells us that this simply is not enough. You must engage with others and involve others to be truly effective. Barack Obama discovered this during his presidential campaign in 2008. One example of his involving approach was that he gave everyone in the US the opportunity to be involved in his campaign by changing the traditional approach to fund raising. Unlike John McCain and other nominees who used public finance for their campaigns, and setting a minimum contribution level from private donors, Obama turned down public finance. He relied wholly on private funding from individual donors who often contributed via the internet. He asked for support from American citizens saying even $5 dollars would help. In the end he raised an amazing $650 million! The net effect speaks for itself and by influencing more people to be personally involved in the process he became the first African American ever to get to the White House, history was made.

Any question that encourages people to open up and offer their opinion, ideas or thoughts on a topic will be helpful. It will contribute to your skill as an influencer and ultimately to gaining others' interest and commitment to your ideas. It is also useful to think about the various question types and those that will be of most use for developing your relationships and influencing others.

The most useful types of question used by successful influencers include:

▍ **Open questions**. These are the simplest form of question to encourage people to think and reflect about a topic, to gather opinions, thoughts and feelings and to give others the opportunity to get involved. Typically open questions begin with – What, why, how, describe. For instance: *What are your views about...? How have you been involved in this project up to now? Tell me more about your thoughts on...?* In answering each of these questions the respondent has the opportunity to offer you their views and to influence your approach to dealing with the issue.

▍ **Probe questions**. This type of question acts as a good follow up to an open question, for instance: *Say a little more? Help me understand by giving me another example? What's your reasoning on this? How do you feel about this?* By encouraging the respondent to explore further and give you even more information you accomplish several things:

   ▍ you can gain greater understanding of the point of view being discussed

   ▍ you can gather more information to help inform the discussion

   ▍ you can demonstrate your real interest in the topic and elicit their views

   ▍ you can involve them in your process

   ▍ you have the opportunity to build on and incorporate their thoughts, ideas or opinions into your outcome.

Several levels of probe questions can be used, by adopting a system often known as funnelling, where you use probe questions to gain more detail and therefore greater understanding about an issue.

▌ **Clarification questions**. These are a good way of testing your understanding and summarising to ensure you have understood the other person's perspective. They also show that you have listened to what has been said. Typically they will go like this: *So, let me just summarise what I think you are saying ...? Can I just clarify ...? Are you suggesting ...? I'd like to make sure I fully understand, What I think you are getting at is ...?*

▌ **Closed questions**. Often badly represented, closed questions do have a purpose and when used effectively can help to ascertain facts and keep control of conversations. Typically, a closed question can be answered with one word or a short phrase. So, for instance when influencing you might use it to control or move on in a conversation, *Does that summary reflect your views? Have I picked up the gist of your argument?*

There is one further questioning technique that is useful for successful influencing. This involves asking more sophisticated versions of those questioning types already mentioned:

▌ **The Socratic technique** – The Socratic questioning technique derives from methods used by the Greek philosopher Socrates. The basic principle relates to challenging and expanding one's thinking and opinion about a subject. So, you would be delving deeper and deeper into the other person's thoughts, views, values, beliefs, rationale, reasoning, assumptions and finally the implications or outcomes that might prevail.

The table on p. 76 gives some examples of this approach:

Success when using questions to assist your influencing process involves certain skills and approaches:

▌ personal commitment to greater understanding

▌ authentic listening and interest in the others' point of view and development of their understanding

THE SOCRATIC TECHNIQUES	
Broadening their thinking.	*Give me an example?* *What exactly are you saying about this?* *Tell me how you know this?*
Challenging their views – as there is always a different perspective.	*So put another way it could be ...,* *How does that seem to you?* *If you compared it to ..., how would that be?* *Let's explore the difference between ... and ...?*
Probing their as yet unquestioned values, beliefs and assumptions about an issue.	*What are you assuming that makes you think that way?* *What would happen if ...?* *How can you back up this assumption?*
Exploring their rationale and reasoning again encouraging deeper thinking and understanding for you both.	*What makes you so sure about this?* *What causes you to think this way?* *What evidence do you have to back up your case?* *How can I be certain of what you are saying?*
Thinking about the future and the implications of their suggestions.	*What might be the consequences of this approach?* *What are the implications of going in this direction?* *How might this work out in the longer term?*

▌ patient inquiry to encourage both your own and their learning

▌ a degree of preparation and planning and a deep knowledge of your subject

▌ curiosity to learn and develop your own awareness and knowledge

▌ a willingness to incorporate their ideas into your plans.

Skilled influencers understand the benefits to be gained from inquiry

Skilled influencers understand the benefits and advantages to be gained from inquiry; they develop their questioning skills and have a genuine inquisitiveness and curiosity to understand others, to be able to incorporate appropriate thoughts, views and ideas into their plans. For example, when you are attempting to convince your team about something isn't it better to involve them by getting their views rather than presenting a fait accompli or even simply stating your views first? In today's busy, chaotic world we tend to feel pushed for time and may forget that, in many situations, influencing involves understanding others' perspectives as well as advocating your own ideas.

Imagine you are in a team meeting with your colleagues discussing the various ideas for reorganising the office space available to you (this has become necessary as you have a couple of new people joining). It would be easy to simply state what you want, possibly adding why and leaving it at that. However, this may not elicit the desired outcome, as people may feel railroaded into something they don't want without having been consulted on their ideas and needs. Influential managers understand that, if you want to build enduring relationships and ensure a motivated workforce with high levels of morale, it is more effective to understand everyone's needs and ideas before presenting your own. So, by developing an inquiry-based approach, when influencing other people, followed by listening, probing and clarification you will know what others want. You will understand how their needs can fit with your ideas, where the gaps are and therefore how much influencing you will have to do.

Basically people want to be heard and asking questions is a magical way of enabling people to share their ideas. Psychologically, the fact that you have asked someone for their opinion goes a long way to developing effective relationships. You may not wholly, or even in a small way, take their ideas on board but often the important thing is that you asked, listened and therefore showed interest.

As the Chinese proverb goes:

> One who asks a question is a fool for five minutes; one who does not ask a question remains a fool forever.

IN SUMMARY ...

In order to develop your quality questioning skills, approaches and techniques you should:

- Notice the types of questions you generally use when in dialogue with others. Ask yourself if these questions elicit the information you require and encourage quality dialogue? If not, you might like to try some new approaches in order that greater understanding and quality of conversation is achieved.

- Plan both the topic and structure of your question prior to any discussion or dialogue. You will then be well prepared, whatever direction the conversation takes.

- Try practising your questions on trusted colleagues; they can then help you test your questioning technique.

- Listen very carefully and use the other person's words to help you frame your questions.

Trust and authenticity

In his book *The Speed of Trust* (2006) Stephen M.R. Covey said that

> Trust is the glue of life. It's the most essential ingredient in effective communication. It's the foundational principle that holds all relationships.

Trust is at the heart of all truly successful relationships. If you don't trust a person or an organisation, then the quality of the relationship will be affected. Indeed, if the quality of the relationship is affected, so too is the performance. It is often the little things, the common courtesies and kindnesses that can make the difference in relationships and help towards building a trusting authentic and open relationship with others. It is so easy to forget the importance of these things. To develop a truly trusting and authentic relationship can take a lifetime and yet that trust can be reduced or even demolished in the blink of an eye.

To develop a trusting relationship can take a lifetime and yet that trust can be demolished in the blink of an eye

FOR INSTANCE

Sonja and James regularly engage in discussions about their work. Sonja confides in James that she is becoming disillusioned with their boss and is applying for jobs outside the organisation. Following a recent discussion Sonja is confronted by her boss who is angry to hear that she is contemplating leaving. From Sonja's perspective she feels let down and betrayed by James. However, James may be unaware of the consequence of what he felt to be a casual conversation.

This will therefore have an effect upon the relationship. It may not lead to a breakdown but will certainly impact on issues such as openness and honesty in the relationship in the future.

Defining trust is a complicated matter, most definitions talk about reliance, integrity, dependence and confidence. For trust to exist in a relationship and for you to be regarded as authentic you need to take into account three things:

▌ instinct – your 'gut' feel about the other person/s

▌ experience – your prior experience of the person/s

▌ clarification – your constant review of the degree of trust between the people in your relationship network

For the purposes of this book we'd like to offer a definition of a trusting and authentic relationship.

A trusting relationship between people is based on each individual's own instincts in relation to authenticity, reliability and integrity about the other/s where both (all) parties can contribute openly and honestly to create a mutually dependent relationship.

Trust and trustworthiness

Trust and trustworthiness are inextricably linked. When you begin a relationship with a person, group of people or an organisation you are always assessing their level of trustworthiness. Typically people use a range of different quite subjective measures to assess whether or not they attribute trustworthiness to a person, group or organisation. These include:

▌ Previous experience of the person, group or organisation

  ▌ Do they keep their promises?

  ▌ Do they take responsibility for actions and outcomes?

  ▌ Are they reliable in delivering on time?

  ▌ Have they ever let you down?

  ▌ Do they treat people fairly?

  ▌ Are they discrete – maintaining confidence?

▌ Other people's views of the person, group or organisation.

  ▌ What do others say about them?

  ▌ Are other's views more positive or negative?

▌ Your view of their intention relating to the situation/event, this is usually based on intuition and instinct and will later be backed by experience.

This assessment of trustworthiness will then contribute towards your views of that person/group/organisation and whether or not you feel you can begin to develop a trusting relationship.

Trust and reputation

Having a trustworthy reputation is critical to business success. So many relationships and opportunities in life are

dependent upon a person, group or organisation having a
positive reputation in order that others will work with them.

A trustworthy reputation is critical to business success

It is said that our reputation precedes us and clearly this
is based on the impressions we give in a wide variety of
situations and also to the various people with whom we
interact. However, like trust, your reputation can easily be
affected by small disappointments. Consequently, you need
to understand what contributes to reputation building and
therefore trustworthiness. Here's another example where
trust and reputation can be called to question.

FOR INSTANCE

Fiona recently had the need to call upon a small training
consultancy to work with a group of colleagues to help them
develop their team working skills. She'd used the consultancy
before and found them to be reliable, friendly and efficient.
Fiona organised an appointment to brief them about her
needs and this meeting went well. They seemed to understand
her needs and promised that they would let her have a brief
proposal with full details of content, costs and dates within
7 days. After a couple of weeks she realised that she had not
received any information from them at all. Fiona called their
office and was told that the person she'd met with had gone
off on holiday and wouldn't be back for another week. She
explained the situation and the person who dealt with her call
was very helpful and promised a 48 hour turnaround on the
proposal (having found the notes on her colleague's desk!).
However, while she's been super efficient, Fiona is still feeling
let down and asks herself, can she trust this consultancy to
deliver a quality event?

Poor reputation can have long lasting consequences for your current and future relationships and indeed your current and future career. In an organisational context, loss of reputation can have a significant effect on the bottom line. Loss of reputation can lead to less business and even closure or bankruptcy. One of the dangers you face is complacency. A little success can go to a person's head, remember trust, trustworthiness and reputation are not about your own feelings in relation to yourself but rather other's perceptions and feelings about you.

Reputation is built on a person's instinct about another person, group of people or organisation's trustworthiness, dependability and authenticity. Once challenged it is difficult to rebuild. In terms of incidents like the example above, you are likely to choose to use someone else in future and also mention it to your network of friends, which will then have a wider affect.

> Reputation is built on a person's instinct about another person, group of people or organisation's trustworthiness

Trust and authenticity

Much is currently made about the concept of authenticity in your work-based relationships. Trust and authenticity go hand in hand, it is difficult to trust someone if you do not regard them as authentic. Like trust, authenticity is difficult to define. When we ask managers what they mean by authenticity in relationship management and influencing, some of the words they use to describe these personality features are:

▌ Integrity	▌ Dependable
▌ Sincerity	▌ Distinctive
▌ Genuine	▌ Compassionate
▌ Trustworthy	▌ Self-disclosing
▌ Principled	▌ Shows respect for self and others
▌ Honest	▌ Acts with goodwill
▌ Consistent	▌ Reliable
▌ Morally upright	▌ Visible

How many of these words would your colleagues use to describe you?

Clearly many of these characteristics can only be determined over a period of time as you get to know a person. It is quite possible for one person to regard you as authentic while another may not. Like many aspects of relationship management this area is subjective and very personal.

When considering authenticity, it is important to recognise that while you have all the best intentions, you have to accept that this is about others' perception of you more than your own self-perception. That said, (as always in this area) how you come across to others starts with your own behaviour.

The sort of behaviour that demonstrates authenticity includes:

▌ standing up for what you believe

▌ being dependable

▌ keeping your promises

▌ communicating with sincerity

▌ admitting your mistakes

▌ operating from an ethical perspective

■ asking others for feedback

■ being natural

■ disclosing information about yourself to others.

Can you add any other behaviours that demonstrate authenticity? How do you think you demonstrate authenticity in your current relationships?

However, it's not just about these behaviours. Demonstrating authenticity is about much more: it's about how you live your life, how you behave when you are with others and generally being true to yourself. Each of us is a unique individual bringing our own personal qualities to bear on all the relationships in our life. How these qualities are received by others will depend upon the other person's prior experience of your behaviour when interacting with them and also how they see you in interactions with others. Reputation also plays a role here, it's not enough to be 'authentic' with certain people and less so with others. Remember people talk to each other and your reputation will often precede you.

Authenticity is about how you live your life

FOR INSTANCE

James – a senior manager had a difficult relationship with his boss. When they were with senior colleagues or with clients, the boss turned into a different person to the person James worked with on a day-to-day basis. With these people he was charming, sociable, asked all the right questions, was patient and, in general, these people found him to be respectful, capable and effective. He worked hard to achieve all his objectives and was, in fact, very good at his job.

However, when he was with peers and more junior colleagues, James believed he saw the true person in action. He was moody, curt and in general pretty disrespectful for a large proportion of the time. The work that James and his colleagues did was high profile, challenging and often pressurised. James recognised that on the whole his boss was good at his job but his relationship skills with many of his colleagues put extra pressure on everyone. James found the whole dual personality issue really challenging and began to resent it.

By using mostly positive behaviour with one group and then adopting a different persona with his colleagues, James's boss was causing real tension in some of his primary relationships at work. This is a typical example of someone who is careless with his relationships at work, does not behave in an authentic way and therefore will not be regarded as being credible and trustworthy with his colleagues. It is certain that eventually his reputation will be negatively affected including his relationship with clients and bosses.

This example or some similar version of it is a common problem that people share with us during coaching or training sessions.

To be a successful relationship leader and manager and influencer, authenticity is a vital quality. People who are authentic and genuine in character are much easier to relate to, as they are more consistent in their behaviour. In general, consistent behaviour makes us feel more certain of people. We like to know what to expect when interacting with others, and when we do, developing an authentic relationship is much easier.

If you are careless about authenticity, you will be putting your reputation and credibility at risk. Your colleagues and staff will be wary about their dealings with you and you certainly will not be getting the most out of the people in your relationship network. At best your relationships will be shallow and superficial.

Carol was pleased with a piece of work her team had been doing and praised and rewarded them. However, her relationship with the team was not all it should have been and some of them doubted her veracity, so while any praise is pleasant to receive the effect was less than it could have been. Had Carol had a better relationship with her team and been regarded by others as an authentic manager, the effect would be more lasting and contribute to a more meaningful and mutually beneficial relationship.

Authenticity also relies to a large extent upon your skill with, and respect for, others. Sometimes we come across people who tell us that 'this is me, take me as I am, I can't change' and they believe that this is being authentic. It may well be, but it's not being skilfully authentic. By skilfully authentic we mean being aware of your own character but behaving flexibly towards others to ensure the relationship is effective for yourself and the others. So, you might like to consider how you demonstrate authenticity in your relationships and how you ensure that your credibility and reputation with others is maintained so that those vital relationships are mutually beneficial.

Trust and distrust

While we have suggested that good relationships are built on a platform of trust, this does not mean that trust always has to exist for a relationship to exist. Trust is primarily necessary for those relationships where you have to rely on another person or group of people in a risky or uncertain situation. In this type of situation, the need for trust is paramount so that you can be sure that the others are not going to let you down.

When distrust exists it is usually due to a previous bad

experience with that person, group or organisation. If this is the case then any relationship that does exist is either casual or transactional in nature, and typically there will be questions about the reliability, ability and dependability of the person and the outcome of any discussion you are having with them.

> ## Distrust is usually due to a previous bad experience with that person

There is of course a middle ground where you neither trust nor distrust the other person/s. This can be the case where the relationship is still developing and you are still assessing your views of the other or it could be that for the situation you find yourself in there is no real need for trust at this stage.

IN SUMMARY ...

So what can you do to give yourself the best possible chance of developing trusting relationships with others – here are some tips.

Do   demonstrate reliability and integrity
keep your promises
display discretion
show appreciation of others
apologise if necessary
ask others for feedback and act on it
take an active interest in others
invest time in getting to know others.

Don't   gossip about others
make promises you cannot keep
fake interest, people see through it
let others down.

Rapport and empathy

Building rapport, being empathetic and showing that empathy to others are key features of effective relationships at work. Far too many of us take rapport and empathy for granted. We want others to be pleasant, considerate and empathetic towards us, but we take much less care in demonstrating these qualities towards others. First, let's look at what we mean by rapport and empathy.

What is rapport?

Rapport is about being in 'synch', or on the same wavelength as the person you are interacting with. It's about being at ease with others and tends to exist most easily with people we are close to or friendly with. You often find that you develop a natural rapport with some people, typically those you are naturally attracted to because they are similar to you in some way. However, like many interpersonal skills, rapport building is capable of development so that you can have rapport even with those people you find initially difficult to relate to.

What is empathy?

There are two stages in being empathetic, firstly, picking up on and secondly, responding to another person's feelings and emotions while you are interacting with them. Clearly it would be a whole lot easier if people would simply tell you how they are feeling. Then you can empathise with them. Sadly, most people do not do tell us how they are feeling. Rather, others expect us to 'read their behaviour' and then to respond appropriately, thus demonstrating empathy. To actively demonstrate empathy you might say, for example:

▌ 'I can see that you are feeling pretty frustrated about this.'

or

▌ 'I understand that this is upsetting for you.'

Or, you may wish to show empathy by a supportive gesture, a smile, a nod, or even a hug, whatever is appropriate for the situation and person.

Demonstrating empathy and building rapport are both skills for which a few people have natural ability. Most of us, however, need to further develop our skill in both areas.

FOR INSTANCE

Mike remembers an experience he had earlier in his consultancy career which highlights the importance of developing rapport. He was applying to undertake a short consultancy project with an international organisation based in the North of France. Obviously he dressed appropriately for a first meeting with this company – suit, shirt, tie, smart shoes and carried a briefcase expecting to have a typically formal business meeting. When he walked into the client's office he was met by a tall Texan who wore no jacket, no tie, shirt sleeves rolled up, sitting with his feet on his desk and wearing a pair of cowboy boots. He introduced himself very informally and motioned to Mike to sit down.

Mike is now faced with a dilemma – how can he establish rapport in a short time period and feel more in synch with the client. So thinking on his feet Mike quickly removed his jacket then as the meeting progressed he loosened his tie, and then rolled up his sleeves to create a better match between his and the client's dress. In addition to this, he decided that rather than presenting his prepared pitch he asked lots of questions to establish what the client was wanting from the relationship. He then listened for speech patterns and language cues and clues so that he could show empathy and then began to flex and structure his pitch to fit with the informal, friendly and relaxed style the client was using.

Empathy, rapport and similar behaviours are of huge importance

Empathy, rapport and similar behavioural approaches are considered to be of huge importance and feature in many of the psychometric and evaluation tools used by organisations around the world for recruitment, performance management and development. Psychologists have identified five dimensions which they call the 'Big 5'. One of the key dimensions of personality described in the 'Big 5' is agreeableness, (the others are: openness, conscientiousness, extraversion and neuroticism), which is described as – consensus oriented, trusting, good natured, co-operative, tolerant, considerate, compassionate and helpful. Companies have recognised that to be a successful people manager you need to be able to demonstrate capability in this area.

Techniques for building rapport and demonstrating empathy

▌ **Self-disclosure**. This involves sharing your feelings and views about topics and personal information about yourself, with others demonstrates an openness and honesty, and leads to a greater ease in rapport building. Self-disclosure enables you to become aware of common interests, ideas, values and beliefs which will in turn enable you to understand more about the other person. When you self-disclose this will often lead to reciprocity where the other person will offer you information about themselves. This level of self-disclosure will then make it easier to show empathy towards others.

Matching and mirroring. These are both Neuro Linguistic Programming (NLP) techniques that you can use to increase your rapport with others which in turn will improve how others perceive you in terms of empathy. Matching means that you closely observe another person's behaviour and then you adapt your behaviour to better match theirs. So, for example, if they are sitting informally, then you sit informally. If they speak slowly and softly, then you match this by speaking more slowly and softly than you usually do. Often when you meet a person you tend to use this technique almost automatically. First, you observe other's body language and voice patterns and then try to adapt your behaviours to more closely match that of the person you are speaking to.

This does not mean that you try to copy their accent or speak exactly the same way as they do. It's more about flexing your own language and body language to be LESS DIFFERENT. Additionally it does NOT mean you mimic someone's words and gestures! If they cross their legs and scratch their nose, you do NOT cross your legs and scratch your nose! That is not matching, but taking the mickey!

FOR INSTANCE

When you are trying to influence colleagues to work with you on a new project, you are more likely to win a hearing if you flex your behaviour then match and pace to work with the other person. So, before you start a conversation with the person reflect about previous conversations with them. Think about:

- their body language
- their vocal tone
- their pace of speech
- their facial expression
- the language they use.

Now plan your conversation bearing all of this in mind.

For example, we know one of our colleagues is confident, formal in his attire, businesslike and contained in his expression and body language. He speaks very quickly, there is an intense feeling about any conversation with him and he tends to be business focussed with a minimal of social chit chat. So when we want to involve him in the project we will organise a time for a formal meeting, send him an agenda prior to meeting, during the meeting we will present our proposal in a confident and businesslike manner. We will express our goals, objectives and timeline. (Typically this would not be our usual way of operating which would be rather more informal, sociable, collaborative, and relaxed.)

In order to develop your ability to match and mirror, the first thing to do is to improve your awareness of others, take some time to observe and listen to others.

▌ Notice how they are standing or sitting.

▌ Take a moment to look around their office if you are in their environment. What do you notice? Is everything neat and tidy or rather informal and haphazard?

▌ How do they speak? Quickly or slowly? Loudly or softly? What kind of words do they use? Can you hear any patterns or buzz words?

Rather than trying to get your point across to them immediately, take the time to notice and become aware of their language and behaviours and then have the flexibility to change your language and behaviours to more closely match theirs.

▌ **Emotional scanning** – first, it is important to tune in to the emotional state of the person/people you are interacting with. Your own emotional antennae should be set to be aware of the prevailing emotional climate within your team, department or organisation. You do this by noticing body language, vocal tone, what people are talking about, and also by asking people 'how they feel'. By taking the time and effort to stand in other people's shoes, not only will you begin to develop a rapport with them, but you will also give yourself resources to help demonstrate empathy.

FOR INSTANCE

One of our clients, the managing director of a small software development company, Ed, is particular good at this. At their Christmas party he mentioned the difficult year the company had had and recognised they would be feeling, angry, sad, frustrated, anxious, because they had lost colleagues and friends through downsizing and the ongoing climate of uncertainty would cause continued anxiety. Most managers would not take the risk of highlighting negative emotions. However, by fully accepting the reality of people's emotional state he has shown himself to be in synch with his colleagues' real feelings. People liked this honesty and humility on his part. In fact, he demonstrated rapport and empathy and, while Ed isn't perfect, his colleagues know that he genuinely cares about both the business and the people.

▍ **Pacing and leading** – are both neuro linguistic programming (NLP) techniques. Pacing involves focussing on the values and habits demonstrated, the content of the conversation and picking up on what the other party is actually saying. Many of the skills involved are similar to those for matching and mirroring; however, pacing and leading are more dynamic. This means that you have to match not only the non-verbal aspects of behaviour but to go deeper into values, words and language. When you pace someone you are acknowledging and respecting their values and culture. For example, when someone says you have 10 minutes for a meeting, accept this and respond to it by getting straight down to business, be quick, direct, focussed and confident. When the 10 minutes are up indicate that you are aware your time is up. If you have established good rapport you will often find that the 10 minutes magically stretches out. Pacing is a prerequisite to moving the conversation forward and beginning to 'lead' towards your goals. By pacing in a conversation you will have used the other person's language and expressions to gain rapport and show empathy.

When you pace someone you are acknowledging their values and culture

FOR INSTANCE

When we work with our Middle Eastern clients we recognise that there are cultural differences in the way we approach day to day work. With many of our Western clients the accepted approach is to work from say nine to six, to have 2 short tea/coffee breaks, an hour for lunch and to switch mobile phones off during sessions. Our experience when working in the UAE indicates a different set of expectations which we have to adapt to. For example, the Arabic day starts earlier and finishes earlier;

> it is not a nine to five culture. Time has to be allocated for prayer breaks, coffee breaks to allow social time and recognising that the family plays an important part in Arabic life. The Arabic culture also seems to be more relationship and socially focussed and therefore some of the processes we typically use when working in the West don't apply in the UAE. The challenge for us is to adapt to the local way of working by pacing with our clients – watching, listening and understanding how they want to work. Having demonstrated our understanding and flexibility by gaining rapport and showing empathy we can then work together to offer suggestions which accommodate both our needs.
>
> If we had just imposed our way of working typically people will conform but the question is will you be developing a sustainable relationship?

Linking and building

The technique is pretty straightforward. It involves being aware of key words the person is using, asking lots of open questions to expand their thinking, listening carefully and looking for areas where you have things in common.

By listening to what the other person has to say you will be more successful. You shouldn't comment, criticise or interrupt. As you listen you must be aware of the key words used, the important words and the words that are repeated. Listen for these key words then reflect them back to the person and probe for more detail to discover the other person's thinking, and explore their thoughts in some depth. That way you start to discover what is behind the other person's idea. You discover their logic, their emotions, their hopes, their fears, their concerns.

An example might be if someone says they are 'concerned' about something, ask them what they mean by 'concern' and what lies behind the word. For some, the word 'concern' is mild. For others when they say 'concern' what they really mean is they are very worried indeed.

Linking and building on aspects of what the other person is saying develops rapport

The skill then is to expand on, link to and build on aspects of what the other person is saying in order to develop rapport. At work we typically make basic statements like 'I think we ought to do x!' To which the normal range of responses are 'I agree!' or 'I disagree!' So when faced with someone saying 'We should do something ...' try to expand their thinking. Force them to give reasons behind the 'ought' or the 'should'. For example, you could say something like 'I agree xxx is a good idea and I'm interested in learning more about your perspective on it, so can we explore that?'

Remember not to judge or criticise as that will just lead to defensiveness and justifications. Expand the other person's thinking by indicating your interest in building or linking and then by asking open questions, like 'What's behind your thinking here?' or 'Can you say a bit more about ...?' Or 'How are you feeling about ...?'

As you gradually expand their thinking you are also forcing them to think and reflect more deeply about their position. Sometimes this can even lead to the person themselves changing their original idea or perspective. You have obliged them to reflect more deeply than they had originally, by indicating interest *without* any criticism or judgement on your part.

What also happens is that you learn a lot by gaining more information and knowledge about the other person's perspective, which will help you to build rapport and develop your relationship with that person.

You can also look for any common areas between your two positions. Clearly, if someone is just saying I think we should do x, there is not much scope for finding things in common, which is why it is important for you to expand the person's thinking, make them reveal more, so that you can then expand the pool of information and more easily find areas of common agreement.

Once you have identified some of these areas of common agreement, then you can start to link these areas together. You are working backwards from potential disagreement to areas where you find that you are in agreement with *some* of what the other person is saying. You are now able to say that you agree with aspects of the other person's position. Psychologically this is important. You are no longer the person who disagrees with everything and who therefore elicits defensiveness and conflict. You may, of course, not agree about anything. However, the chances of this are minimised if you go through the process described above.

FOR INSTANCE

Harold and John work for a small company which runs training courses for managers.

In a meeting about a people skills course for a group of senior managers in the telecommunications industry Harold proposes spending more time on the programme on the subject of Time Management. John disagrees with Harold here, but instead of just saying 'I disagree!' and then expounding his own position, what he does is bite his tongue. (Usually, he's a bit of a habitual criticiser) He asks Harold to elaborate on his reasons for wanting to do this. Harold then explains that he feels that delegation is a critical aspect of Leadership, and he feels that if managers do not have a good sense of managing time effectively they would be unable to delegate effectively.

Now John disagrees that they should spend more time on Time

Management as a subject, but he does fully agree with Harold that delegation is a key aspect of Leadership. This enables John and Harold to move away from disagreement to partial agreement. John explicitly says to Harold that he agrees with him that he is absolutely right that delegation is important and is a key aspect of leadership and that Time Management is a part of delegation. Now we have some positive dynamic in the conversation. Psychologically speaking, John has not upset Harold, or provoked defensiveness and justification. They are now in agreement on a higher level. Of course there is still a level of disagreement, specifically on how much time should be spent on Time Management, but the climate of the discussion is now positive. The disagreement is seen to be at a lower level. Harold also feels he has been listened to, feels respected and taken seriously.

The next bit of the conversation can be about how much time to give to Time Management. It's now up to John to expand again on Harold's thinking. What does Harold feel is the essential aspect of TM? What is absolutely vital? What is the key message that Harold wants to get across to participants?

The conclusion of the meeting is that Harold can talk about TM in the seminar, but that it will be clearly linked to delegation and leadership and he will only give some key aspects of TM rather than spending several hours on it.

IN SUMMARY ...

As we have seen, developing rapport and empathy are critical for effective leadership in business. Here are a few summary points from the chapter:

- Try not to jump immediately to disagreement and then propose your own perspective or opinion on a subject.
- Remember to ask open questions.
- Expand the other person's thinking.
- Notice what they say and how they say it.
- Look for things in common and potential areas of agreement.
- Build on these areas.

How to become more self- and others aware

Knowing others is wisdom, knowing yourself is Enlightenment.

Lao Tzu

Effective managers recognise the importance of self awareness. It helps you to understand who you really are and why you do the things you do, in the way that you do them. It is an essential element for effective interpersonal relationships and for good communication. Self-awareness, however, is only one part of the equation. Reading and observing other people to pick up on the cues and clues they give you about their feelings, emotions and moods will help you to be even more successful when developing relationships and influencing others.

Self-awareness

Most of you will be content with your relationships when things are going well, and when you can use your interpersonal skills in a confident and appropriate manner. However, when things go wrong, or difficulties arise, when you feel challenged, stressed or find yourself in an unfamiliar situation, you will find that you have to look for ways to approach things differently. You will have to use approaches that you find less comfortable, and you may therefore, use them in a less confident and capable way. This is when good self-awareness comes into its own. The more you understand yourself, the more you will be able to assess how best to communicate and work with others in a confident and appropriate way.

> The more you understand yourself, the more you will be able to communicate and work with others

Here are some ideas about how to develop your self-awareness:

- Begin by asking yourself some questions and noting down the answers (See chart on p. 103).

- Ask people for feedback (see Chapter 15 for guidance on this) and note down responses and your reactions to them.

- Try to fill in some personality questionnaires – for instance: The Myers Briggs Type Indicator (MBTI), Fundamental Interpersonal Relationships Orientation – Behaviour (FIRO-B), Strength Deployment Inventory (SDI), and Belbin Team Roles Questionnaire. What do they tell you about your personality, are there any common messages that stand out? How do they relate to your own identification of your strengths and weaknesses?

- Think about the performance reviews you have had with your line manager, and not just the current one. Reflect back over your whole working life. What information about yourself can you gain from these to help you raise your self-awareness?

- Think about yourself in different situations, for instance, group meetings, discussions with your boss, confrontational discussions and presentations. Now

What are my strengths?	
What are my weaknesses?	
What are my potential blind spots?	
What do I enjoy doing, what motivates me?	
What do I not enjoy doing, what demotivates me?	
How might my friends, family, colleagues describe me?	
What qualities, skills and abilities do I see in others that I would like to have myself?	
What are my dreams and ambitions for the future?	
What are my values and beliefs for life?	

consider how you feel about each of these different types of interaction. How do you behave (think about your body language, vocal tone, content of your message) and how do you respond to others when interacting with them in such situations?

▌ Practise putting yourself in the other person's shoes before different interactions. Ask yourself how they might be feeling, what they might expect from you in terms of behaviour, content and outcome. Think about how they might be interpreting your behaviour, feelings and intentions during the interaction.

Analysing yourself

Being self-aware and developing yourself takes time, and many of you will need a structure to help in this area. One such approach which has become accepted as a useful tool to help you to understand, reflect about and help you plan how best to raise your self-awareness was developed back in 1955 by psychologists Joseph Luft and Harry Ingham and it remains extremely relevant today. They developed this system to help people think about their interpersonal relationships – they called it 'The Johari Window'. They suggested that there were aspects of your personality that you tend to be open about and other elements you keep to yourselves. There are also things that others see in you that you are not aware of. Finally, there is also an area of you that everyone is unaware of.

▌ **Your public self**. The things you know about yourself and others know about you based on the behaviour you use in interpersonal relationships.

▌ **Your blind spots**. The things others know about you but you do not know. This relates to the behaviour you use and the interpretation others put on it and you remain unaware of its impact.

▌ **Your hidden self**. The things you know about yourself but

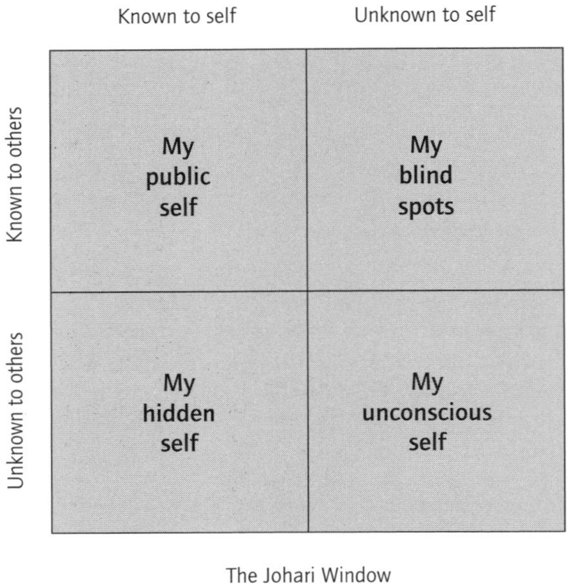

	Known to self	Unknown to self
Known to others	My public self	My blind spots
Unknown to others	My hidden self	My unconscious self

The Johari Window

Figure 11.1 The Johari Window

Luft and Ingham 1955

others do not know. This can be things you prefer not to reveal about yourself because they are sensitive.

▌ **Your unconscious self.** The things that neither you nor others know about you. Usually related to behaviour and motives that you haven't used.

As part of your development about your own self-awareness you should reflect about the relative size of each of the 4 areas in the Johari Window. Perhaps you can think about this with reference to the different relationships you have both at work and in your social life. To help you with your reflection you can follow the general guidelines below:

▌ A large public self would indicate that you are open and self-disclosing. You are willing to share a lot of yourself with others, and you will have had feedback from others to confirm that you have formed an accurate picture of yourself.

▌ A large blind spot area would indicate that you are not aware of how others see you, you are unaware of the impact you have on others and may be regarded as lacking in self-awareness.

▌ A small public self, large blind spot and large hidden self would indicate that you tend to be a very private person who keeps things to themselves and rarely discloses personal information and feelings to others.

▌ In order to increase your public self and decrease your blind self, you will need to ask others for feedback, or, indeed, be open to feedback that is offered to you by others. First, you have to accept the feedback then act on it. The only real way you will increase self-awareness is to demonstrate change and do something about the feedback you get.

▌ In order to increase your public self and decrease your hidden self you need to offer more information about yourself to others by sharing new information of which others were previously unaware.

▌ As you grow and develop, take on new responsibilities and take part in new experiences you will have the opportunity to explore your unconscious self and to continue increasing your public self by finding out new things about yourself.

Effective relationship leaders and managers understand that you can always be building and developing self-awareness. They recognise that new people and situations provide opportunities for finding out even more about yourself. In order to be truly self-aware you have to be open to new ideas, new opportunities and to reflecting about what you are learning from these situations that will help you to be effective and successful in all your working relationships. As US Tennis Champion, Billie Jean King says:

I think self-awareness is probably the most important thing towards being a champion.

Awareness of Others

The other half of the awareness story relates to other people and largely depends upon your skills of observation and analysis. Skillful observers are good listeners and people watchers. You will also be good at reading people and situations as well as recognising the signs, signals and patterns of behaviour others use.

> Skillful observers are good listeners and people watchers

Skillful observers have a genuine interest in, are available to and curious about people. They will be approachable, have learned to recognise the cues and clues others give as to their moods, emotions, feelings and thoughts and will have developed the capacity to adapt their behaviour to suit the people and situations. They take the time to be with others in all sorts of different environments and situations. They will also have a generally optimistic outlook, trying to see the positive in people, in order to find ways of relating to them in a constructive and encouraging way.

Reading people takes time and effort. It is a process of assessment, where you are watching and appraising others, making judgements about their emotional attitude and developing hypotheses about them based on current and past experience of working with them. In addition to planning your behaviour this can also help you to understand more about your colleagues' drivers and motivations. This will add to your knowledge about them and ultimately help you to develop good working relationships. You can then use this to plan your behaviour and approach when dealing with that person or group.

FOR INSTANCE

You have recently been promoted to a senior management position within your own organisation but at a different office. Like all new jobs getting to know the new team is a challenge. During the first few weeks you have been focussing on getting to know your three direct reports, Sarah, Asif and Max, all of whom are line managers in their own right. You have now had several one-to-one and a range of group meetings with them and so far you have noticed that:

- **Sarah** is chatty, speaks quickly, is quite relaxed in her posture, asks a lot of questions and involves the others at group meetings by inviting them into the conversation by asking for their point of view. She is well respected by her team and tends to manage in an involving and consultative way. She has been very helpful during your first few weeks in the new role and has helped you to understand much about the division you are now heading up.

- **Asif** is more challenging; he is low key and much more difficult to read. You have noticed that he plays his cards close to his chest, listens to what's going on around him before he offers his own opinions or ideas. In your one-to-one meetings with him he is concise and to the point and you get the impression he is holding back somewhat. You have also noticed that even with his team he can be a little distant, so at least it's not just reserved for you.

- **Max** is prickly; he has opinions and views on most things about the work of the division and the organisation and doesn't listen a lot to the others, often interrupting and showing impatience in meetings. In his one to ones with you he is always in a rush and it has been pretty difficult to entice information from him. He seems to want to run his own show without any interference. He is however excellent at his job, a hard worker and has his team behind him. You also know that he was interviewed for the role you eventually got.

You know that you will have to continue to pick up clues and cues as you try out different ways of operating with them to develop effective working relationships and to help you decide on the best approaches for each one. But, even now all three have given you sufficient information for you to begin to develop your relationship with each:

- **Sarah** – her behaviour suggests to you that she wants to be involved and to feel useful to you and others. Your approach will be to ensure you involve her, ask her opinion, test ideas out with her and work with her to help you develop your relationship with the others.

- **Asif** – seems to be a shyer person. You notice he needs time to consider issues and works better with facts than opinion or emotion. So, you know that you will have to take your time with him. For a start you will have to provide him with data and then allow him time to think things through before you engage in discussion. You suspect working with him will feel more formal than your relationship with Sarah.

- **Max** – is going to be the biggest challenge for you. Quite apart from the feelings he may have from his lack of success in getting the job he is also the one who you believe is most like you. So, you know that with him there is potential for conflict. Your plan for Max is to ask his opinion, give him challenges, set clear objectives and generally give him freedom to operate. You will however, establish ground rules including reporting procedures.

These are your thoughts so far and you know that as each relationship develops you will continue to find out more about each of them which in turn will lead to new ideas.

IN SUMMARY ...

High self-awareness means that you are in close contact with the reality of how people see you. This gives you the self-knowledge necessary to know when it's appropriate to adapt and adjust your behaviour to suit others' needs. Self-awareness helps you to determine how best to flex your individual approach to be confident, in control and use appropriate behaviour for the people you are communicating with in any given situation. Low self-awareness means that there is a danger of becoming disconnected with the reality of others' perceptions of you. This leads to an inability to read situations and respond appropriately to others.

Others' awareness requires an open mind and a willingness to adapt your behaviour, it may even mean operating out of your comfort zone in order to develop strategies and approaches for creating and building effective working relationships. Without awareness of yourself and others, you cannot be aware of the dynamics of the relationships and the helpful and unhelpful patterns that exist. Success rests with building on helpful behaviours and altering unhelpful ones. You will find more detail about these in the following chapters.

Emotional awareness and management

Earlier in this book we established that emotional connection is one of the key elements to enable fully formed high quality engaging and influential relationships to develop and flourish. So, emotional awareness and management are important elements of the engagement and relationship management needed by leaders and managers. Learning to understand, master and regulate your emotions will help you to contribute to the creation, development and effectiveness of your relationships at work. This will ultimately ensure that you become an effective leader and influencer in your business and social environment.

Emotional awareness and management is key

Emotional awareness was popularised in business in the 1990s following the publication of Daniel Goleman's book *Emotional Intelligence: Why it can matter more than IQ*. Of course the concept of emotional intelligence was not new; psychologists and thinkers have recognised the importance of emotions in day-to-day life for centuries. Carl Gustav Jung acknowledged this in the early twentieth century, stating that:

> There can be no transforming of darkness into light and of apathy into movement without emotion.

Cicero (106BC–43 BC) recognised it even earlier:

> Men decide far more problems by hate, love lust, rage, sorrow, joy, hope, fear, illusion or some other inward emotion, than by reality, authority, any legal standard, judicial precedent or statute.

Most events in our life will trigger feelings and emotions and these feelings and emotions will lead to thoughts and behaviours which will be used in our interactions with others. Becoming more aware of the emotions and feelings and the response we have to them is all part of emotional awareness. Our definition of emotional awareness is 'recognition of the psychological and physiological state associated with a wide variety of *feelings*, *thoughts*, and *behaviour*.' Emotional awareness and management is a truly soft skill but it is tremendously hard for some people to master. Success depends on 5 key factors:

- noticing and naming your emotions and feelings
- understanding the messages your emotions are conveying to you and the impact these feelings have on your emotional response and behaviour towards others
- how you demonstrate the emotion or feeling to others
- how your demonstration of any emotion affects others
- development of the capability to regulate, manage and adapt your emotional responses appropriately. This is especially important in a working environment.

All of these factors will have a significant effect on your success when engaging with and relating to others. Mastery of your emotions can only make you a better relationship manager.

Noticing and naming emotions

People find it extremely challenging to recognise their emotions, naming and sharing them provides an even bigger issue for them. Having the capability to understand your own emotions and to be able to talk with others about them will pay huge dividends when influencing and managing relationships at work as well as in your personal life. One of the first tests for many of us is recognising and naming our emotions and feelings. The following table lists some of the more common emotions expressed to us during conversations with managers and business executives.

People find it challenging to recognise their emotions

A brief list of emotions		
Love	Fear	Disappointment
Worry	Contempt	Rage
Frustration	Delight	Appreciation
Sadness	Hostility	Impatience
Anger	Joy	Annoyed
Sorrow	Hurt	Betrayal
Envy	Pity	Undervalued
Surprise	Upset	Apprehensive
Anxiety	Energised	Positive
Disgust	Anticipation	Relief
Enthusiasm	Jealousy	Pleased
Excitement	Indignation	Thrilled
Desire	Loathing	Doubtful
Horror	Misery	Negative

Clearly this is not an exhaustive list as there are literally thousands of different emotions and feelings. However, one way of becoming more aware is to take time to reflect when you are interacting with others in a variety of different situations and put a name to the emotion or feeling, this is called signalling. The simple action of being able to reflect about, and signal to others your internal emotional state, for instance: 'I feel angry', I feel excited about...', 'this makes me feel disappointed', can improve your effectiveness when in dialogue with others. From a relationship development and influencing perspective, stating how you are feeling by naming your emotional state will help people to more clearly understand your message and point of view.

> ### FOR INSTANCE
>
> You meet with your team to chat through a new project that you are all going to be involved in over the coming months. The purpose of the meeting is to inform them about the project and their role in it and the timescale and key result areas. Now, you could take a factual stance and simply explain the objective, go through the time line, establish their role and responsibilities and set priorities. OR You could open your meeting by talking about your excitement and how this opportunity will provide the whole team with the opportunity to demonstrate their capability and build their credibility before you go into any detail about the project other than the overall objective. Typically people who can express their own emotions and feelings in this type of situation will engage with a wider audience than those who only operate at a factual level.

Understanding Your Emotions or Feelings

There is a big difference between recognising your emotions and actually understanding the impact they have on you. We all demonstrate our emotional response and feelings about an issue in different ways. Sometimes these demonstrations can support our case. For example, enthusiastic excitement about a new opportunity can be infectious and can lead to interesting discussion and debate about the issue where everyone is involved and listened to. However, if people have different perspectives they can come at a problem in different ways. The way you present yourself emotionally can be a major turn off if inappropriate for the person or situation you are dealing with. The example below illustrates one case of lack of personal awareness leading to ineffective influencing and relationship management.

The way you present yourself emotionally can be a major turn off

FOR INSTANCE

A manager we worked with on a recent assignment wanted ideas to help him to be more influential in meetings with his colleagues on the board. This objective is not unusual and there can be many reasons why people want to develop in this area. It became clear rather quickly what one of his problems was. In a team exercise where the participants all started from slightly different perspectives and had to reach a workable compromise, Robert changed from being a rather affable, chatty and friendly character who expressed genuine interest in others to someone who:

- spoke very quickly and loudly with greater emphasis on certain words when he wanted to make a point

- used gestures like finger pointing, finger drumming, fist beating on table

- sulking and disengaging when not being listened to. Such as, playing with his blackberry, which is regarded as a sign of disengagement.

- on occasions became quite critical about colleagues' approach to an issue if it differed from his.

Fortunately, this exercise was recorded onto DVD to aid in the feedback process so we were able to show Robert how he behaved in the meeting. During our analysis to draw out the learning Robert was quite upset and seemed genuinely unaware that his behaviour changed to such an extent. This awareness alone was a major learning point for him. However, when we asked what he was feeling and what his emotions in the meeting were, he was able to say he felt frustrated when others kept offering new ideas, then ignored when others would not explore his ideas and finally downright angry when they began to ignore him. The real breakthrough however was when Robert began to talk about other difficult relationships and the realisation that this was a pattern of behaviour which was in response to others when they didn't accept and explore his views with him. He concluded 'no wonder people are wary of me'.

Recognising and naming his emotions followed by the opportunity to view himself in action made Robert realise the impact the emotions were having on his behaviour (and on his relationships with others). Not everyone has the benefit of a training course with recording equipment, but you can take more time to review your relationships and reflect about your emotions and feelings in different situations. In particular, you can begin to identify situations that stir up negative emotions for you which can lead to difficult relationship issues. It is also worth thinking about the situations where you have positive emotions and where your behaviour is supportive to your relationships. Greater awareness and understanding in these areas will help you to plan and prepare to ensure more effective outcomes when interacting with and influencing others.

Reflect or ask others for feedback about your behaviour in different situations and begin to understand the situations, people or behaviours that trigger positive and negative emotional responses.

Ask others for feedback about your behaviour

Begin to think through how you can deal with these emotions in a more effective manner. Are your emotions:

▌ **Person specific**. Do certain people or personality types affect your emotional reactions?

▌ **Behaviour specific**. Are certain behaviours like lack of listening, interrupting, bad language, belligerence, affecting your emotional responses?

▌ **Situation specific**. Do certain situations like conflict or having to talk at big meetings affect how you feel and how you demonstrate these feelings?

How You Demonstrate Your Emotions

Recognising your internal emotional responses is just the beginning. It is also important to recognise and understand how your outward behaviour changes. Your raised awareness of your emotional behaviour will help you to be more aware of the external behavioural changes, for instance:

▌ changes in your voice – speed, pitch, tone, language usage

▌ changes in body language – hand and arm gestures, stance, posture, facial expression

▌ changes in your communication style – interrupting, challenging, advocating, silence, supporting

▌ changes in your way of expressing yourself – using stronger language, becoming critical, becoming defensive, attacking, enthusing

▌ showing excitement, enthusiasm, energy

▌ disengaging and appearing to sulk.

Whatever you do it is important to be more aware of how your behaviour changes when communicating with others. Why not use that digital video camera or your mobile phone to record yourself in discussion with others. Then replay and critically review your own behaviour after the meeting to check for those subtle and not so subtle changes. People

are often unaware of changes in facial expression, eye
contact, language and tone. All of which have an effect upon
your relationships with others and your ability to influence
effectively. The single most successful way to understand
how you demonstrate your emotion is to ask others. Perhaps
start by asking a trusted colleague or friend for feedback
or get into the habit of asking people for feedback on your
body language, and the impact and impression you create in
various situations. (More tips on feedback in Chapter 15.)

Critically review your own behaviour

Regulating your emotions

The whole purpose of emotional awareness and management
is to be more emotionally and socially intelligent, so that you
can use your emotions in a positive and constructive manner
when influencing and interacting with others. Your emotions
will have a major impact upon others and the relationship
they develop with you. It is important to recognise the
impact your differing emotions have on different people in
your relationship network. Here are some tips for regulating
and managing your emotions for interpersonal success:

- **Stay calm, and count to ten before responding** to someone
  when you feel your emotions are sweeping you away into
  an unhelpful place. Then follow with a question.

- **Learn to recognise your emotional triggers** – those
  situations, people and behaviours that prompt your own
  inappropriate emotional behaviour.

- **Develop a script** – once you recognise situations,
  people and behaviour that lead to what you believe to
  be unhelpful emotional responses. Examples might be,
  showing anger, losing control or using inappropriate
  language. You can then develop new scripts. For example:

ask a question rather than continue to argue, thank the
person for their point of view, then move on to indicate
that you disagree and you'd like to share your perspective
with them.

FOR INSTANCE

A group of media trainers we have worked with told us about
their work with a group of French politicians who wanted to
be more effective in debate when attempting to influence
people. The trainers observed that most of the politicians were
passionate about their beliefs and demonstrated this when
debating by openly expressing their views in a passionate
and energetic way. Their speech was fast, loud and extremely
expressive. Their body language was dramatic with strong and
powerful hand and arm gestures. The trainers felt that while
this technique worked for formal speeches it was overpowering
and off-putting in debate. They suggested that when debating
or inviting opinion or contribution from others it might help to
adopt the 'count to ten' rule followed by a question technique.
This, together with more controlled body language, for
instance, steepling of the hands proved to be more effective
when influencing and engaging with others. By counting to
ten they not only slowed down their own behaviour but also
demonstrated a willingness to listen. The follow-on question
demonstrated interest in others' opinions.

▌ **Rehearse beforehand** – especially if you know that there
is a high possibility of inappropriate emotional response.

▌ **Reframe the situation** – try to understand it from the other
person's perspective so that you then respond differently.
(See Chapter 18 on Reframing.)

▌ **Write about your emotional responses to situations** –
getting into the habit of writing a reflective diary can be
very useful to help you name, notice, understand your
reactions and identify situations that make you react

inappropriately. This can then lead to greater awareness and ultimately better emotional regulation.

The relationally aware manager realises that emotional awareness is about recognition and self-control. It is not about suppressing your emotions, but rather about using them in effective and appropriate ways. Your goal is to develop your soft skills to become more relationally intelligent, engaging and influential.

Emotional awareness is about recognition and self-control

IN SUMMARY ...

Emotional awareness and management are both important qualities for successful relationship management. To be successful in this area you should develop the capability to:

- Notice and name the emotions you experience in different situations.

- Analyse and understand your internal emotional responses to people, events and situations.

- Be aware of your emotional behaviour towards others and the impact it has.

- Regulate your emotions by recognising your emotional triggers and responding appropriately.

Being politically astute

O ften regarded as a negative element of life in organisations, politics are, in fact, an inherent part of it. The influential leader recognises this and accepts that it is necessary to learn how to operate within and understand this political arena. There is however, a huge difference between being political and being politically astute. In this chapter we will explore the part politics plays as an element of an influential leader's role. In particular, we will explore what organisational politics involves, and the various approaches people take to managing the political environment in their organisation.

Politics are a part of life in organisations

Organisational Politics

Since in all organisations there is an element of politics, it is clearly worth considering what type of political arena you are operating in. The descriptions below highlight three levels of organisational politics. You might like to use this to determine the political landscape in your organisation or your part of the organisation:

▌ **Minor political landscape** – organisations where there is a sense of camaraderie, collegiality, and team work is valued, rewarded and celebrated, and there is a high level of trust and respect between colleagues. Open conflict is rare as any disagreement is typically sorted out through discussion. Managers will operate within the organisational rules and norms with minimal rule bending. These are often small/medium-sized organisations where everyone knows everyone else. This type of organisation is increasingly rare in today's business world, but will exist in pockets in many organisations.

▌ **Moderate political landscape** – organisations where in general managers operate within the rules, but where individual managers and departments may have invented their own 'rules' for getting things done. People in these organisations tend to be rewarded for individual success and different departments can operate in different ways. This type of political landscape often exists when an organisation is rapidly growing and going through significant change where risks need to be taken and rules need to be challenged.

▌ **Highly political landscape** – organisations where there is a sense of competition, lots of cliques and in and out groups. Gossip and rumour mills are rife, and conflict between and within departments is common. Rules and processes in this type of organisation are a convenience often ignored and certainly not applied consistently. In organisations of this type there will certainly be individuals who are clearly in the 'inner circle' and one must be wary not to upset them.

You may feel that within your organisation all three landscapes exist and this is quite possible.

Manoeuvring the political landscape in your organisation involves using discretionary behaviours and approaches to get things done. It's about going outside the normal practices and processes to achieve goals and objectives. Politics can be good or bad for an organisation, and this will depend upon how managers deploy their skills to operate within the political arena. Political skill in the main is about how managers behave when pursuing their organisational goals.

Politics can be good or bad for an organisation

There are four main types of organisational politician. Those who avoid getting involved in the politics in their organisation, we call them the *politically virtuous*. Those who are unaware of organisational politics and much of it passes them by are *politically naive*. Others are highly involved and are what we term *political operators*. These are the managers who manipulate the system to get what they want. Finally there are influential leaders and managers who understand that politics are an inevitable aspect of organisational life, and appreciate you have to operate within the political arena while also maintaining your integrity, credibility and reputation with your colleagues. These people are the *politically astute*.

The Politically Virtuous

People who choose not to or won't get involved in organisational politics because they see this as immoral and distasteful, they believe they are above all of this kind of political behaviour. Managers who fall into this category believe that taking part in organisational politics is unethical and unnecessary. They think getting things done and getting on in business is about doing your job well, following the established rules and processes within the organisation and trusting others to do the same. These people often get left behind and wonder why promotion is not forthcoming. Sometimes virtuous types choose to leave organisations where there is a highly political environment, as they simply can't operate in this type of culture.

Typical behavioural patterns for the politically virtuous are that they:

▌ obey and work by the rules and expect others to do so as well

▌ regard organisational politics with distaste and tell people so, having little regard for others who operate in a political manner

▌ want to know what's expected of them and by when

▌ value openness and honesty and have a tendency to tell people as it is

▌ work hard and believe they will be rewarded for this, as they believe that progression is about hard work and competence.

The Politically Naive

Managers who are politically naive are idealists who are oblivious to the political landscape around them. They tend to trust their colleagues to be honest and open and believe that everyone is focussing on the same goals. These people are often surprised by some colleagues who are more successful and climb the organisational career ladder more speedily. When they analyse the reasons it isn't always about good performance. They discover that some people are promoted because they know the 'right' people, or they've done a favour for someone in the past and now it's payback time. Or, in some cases someone has simply played an unfair game and taken credit for something that wasn't wholly their own work.

Managers who are politically naive will operate within the organisational rules and processes; they will work together with others to create conditions that are favourable to all.

They tend to be natural team players who genuinely want to perform to their best and to be supportive to the team, their colleagues and the organisation. Managers who operate in this way are those who, if willing, can develop into influential managers who operate in a politically astute way.

Typical behaviours of the politically naive are:

- people oriented and often team players who see the best in all people
- usually quite sociable and liked by others
- underplay own achievements in favour of the team's or organisation's
- may be regarded as gullible by others.

The Political Operator

The political operator is the most challenging of the political types. These managers are political game players who pursue their own individual agenda in a self-interested manner. They take no notice of the impact or effect they are having on others, or indeed on the organisation and its efforts to achieve its goals and objectives. We have called this approach 'political operator' and regard it as destructive behaviour in the long term. It is this type of behaviour that contributes to giving organisational politics a bad name.

> Political operators tend to be self-interested

Managers who are political operators tend to be self-interested individuals. They use parochial, selfish and divisive approaches in service of their own ends in relation to their organisational goals and objectives. They are often referred to as political operators by others in their organisation and are regarded with suspicion and wariness.

You may have identified these people because you have been caught out or tripped up by them at some point.

Initially, this type of manager can appear to be interpersonally skilled, involving and authentic; it is usually after the event that you discover they have acted in their own self-interest. Political operators are clever, persuasive and in many cases they appear to be successful by reaching senior levels in organisations. However, as in the example below, when it becomes clear they have been acting from self-interest and manipulating their colleagues, they will be regarded with suspicion by others and ultimately this can lead to derailment at some point in the future.

FOR INSTANCE

Being political

You are part of a project team charged with developing a new customer service process. You know that this is an important project for your organisation's future success and that the whole team are under the spotlight as the new process will require a new manager. So, there may be an opportunity for a promotion for one of you. You are all aware of this possibility. However, you have discussed it and agreed to operate as a team allowing the promotion possibility to take its own course.

Towards the end of the project, just before you all report your findings to the board, you notice Nina, one of your team-mates coming out of the Chief Executive's office. Later that day you mention it to her and she shrugs it off saying she was just confirming the agenda for the presentation to the board.

During the presentation it becomes clear from his questions and comments that the CE knows quite a bit about your recommendations. You remember about Nina and have some suspicions that she may not have simply been going through the agenda! A month later your suspicions are confirmed when she is offered the management role. While you can't prove anything

> you feel rather less trusting towards Nina and will be very cautious in future when working with her.
>
> In this case Nina was playing a political game and you were being somewhat politically naïve. A more politically astute person might have made sure that they contacted the Chief Executive prior to the meeting to confirm that the team's understanding of the agenda is the same as his. Additionally, when you saw Nina leaving the Chief Executive's office you might have been rather more sceptical.

Typical behavioural patterns used by 'political operators' include:

- making friends with people in influential positions
- supporting the 'right' cause and the 'right' people
- attacking and blaming others
- denying involvement in negative events
- hoarding information and keeping it from others then using it to promote own position
- creating alliances and coalitions by appearing to agree with others then using these alliances to meet own selfish ends
- self-promotion by overplaying accomplishments and abilities and enhancing achievements
- taking credit for other peoples' work.

Most of you will be able to identify people you work with or have worked with who behave in some or all of these ways. Sadly, there will always be people around who think it's OK to win at all costs no matter what the consequences might be. The issue for influential leaders is not to fall into this trap and to learn to deal with political operators by developing your own political skill.

The Politically Astute

The politically astute leader uses their discretionary behaviour to achieve their objectives in a more inclusive way. They take account of others' needs and wants and are constantly striving to align with the organisational goals. They are leaders who recognise and understand that organisational politics are a fact of life. They develop and use their skills and behaviours in pursuit of organisational goals and recognise their own and others' needs.

Truly influential leaders recognise the importance of the political environment within their organisation and aim to work with it. They manage their behaviour accordingly. Being politically astute is a complex process which involves awareness, willingness and a sophisticated use of your interpersonal skill set.

> Influential leaders recognise the importance of the political environment

Typical behavioural patterns used by the politically astute are the ability to:

- flex and adapt both leadership and relationship style to suit the people and the situation

- demonstrate awareness of your own personal strengths and weaknesses and how best to capitalise on the strengths and avoid situations which will draw upon the weaker areas

- work with both the people and the problem in a way that brings about positive and beneficial outcomes

- focus on both the here and now and the future. They understand the importance of working effectively in the moment and being aware of where they want to be in the future

▌ manage by wandering around and getting to know and appealing to the people who operate within their political landscape. They are avid networkers – not with any Tom, Dick or Harry but rather a planned development of their network focussed around those who can help, support and be useful now and in the future

▌ develop trust and respect from others by recognising others, asking for help or support when necessary. Rewarding others appropriately and generally understanding that their credibility rests on their recent behaviour. Recognising that it can be lost very easily and once gone is hard to regain

▌ develop good quality relationships with trusted others so that they always have people to test their ideas on, to act as a sounding board and who will keep them connected with other parts of the organisation.

IN SUMMARY ...

Jeffrey Pfeffer said 'Management is itself a political activity' and it is certainly a hard fact of contemporary business life. Influential leaders and managers alike learn to operate within political organisations. The successful people expend time and energy to develop their political skills and capabilities and aim to use these skills to help both themselves and their organisation to be successful. Of course, it is your choice as to whether you use your skills with integrity and authenticity to develop as a politically astute player who becomes well respected and trusted. Or you could choose not to play politics, recognise that you need to play, or worst of all choose to win at all costs.

Finally, as Winston Churchill said 'When you mix people and power you get politics' so politics are inevitable wherever you work.

How to handle conflict

14

Conflict and confrontation are unavoidable in both our personal and organisational lives, so the skill is to accept that conflict will happen. However, how you handle conflict with your colleagues at work will have an enormous impact on the way you are perceived as a manager. Conflict has both its good and bad points. If dealt with well, it can spark new ideas and encourage improvements in communication and relationships, but if dealt with badly, it can lead to relationship breakdown and bad feeling between people. It is therefore important to learn how to deal with conflict and confrontation in a positive and effective way!

Conflict has its good and bad points

Types of Conflict

There are many different types of conflict or reasons why conflict arises. We have categorised it into two broad types – Personal and Organisational.

Personal Conflict

Personal differences of opinion caused by differing sets of

values, beliefs, perceptions or expectations are probably the most common cause of any conflict or confrontation, whether inside or outside the work environment. These differences tend to be either person or issue based. Person based conflict arises when your feelings and emotions have been affected by negative personal interaction. An issue based conflict tends to be less emotive, it is less likely to be personally motivated but more about an event or situation.

Misunderstanding and misinterpretation of meaning when you are communicating with other people is another common cause of conflict. Whether communication is verbal or in writing (email, memo, text) it is very easy for each person to interpret things in a different way, and reach different conclusions which can then lead to misunderstanding.

FOR INSTANCE

We are often told stories about misunderstandings and misinterpretation caused by poor use of language on emails which leads to confrontation.

Rachel showed us an email she had received from a colleague. Her reaction to the email was very negative. She had interpreted the language and tone used by the writer as critical of her behaviour, as her colleague had used accusatory, emotive and negative language such as *'Sadly it smacks of you not being up to this'*, *'imagine how this is looking to others'* and *'with all due respect my friend'*. These are all irritators, which will undoubtedly engender a negative reaction, which will lead to conflict.

As it turns out the writer of the email has a track record of using this type of language in emails without thinking of how other people will interpret them and the subsequent consequences.

The lesson here is to be aware that when writing emails, memos or texts, that the lack of visual and vocal clues make it difficult to assess the recipient's response so care must always be taken to consider the quality of the content and potential reactions to it.

Working within a stressful or pressurised culture can also cause conflict between individuals. Some of you will thrive on pressure and be able to operate effectively in that kind of environment. Not everyone is able to cope with pressure and for many people pressure is counterproductive causing them to become demotivated. So it is important to take account of your own and others' levels of tolerance to pressure and stress.

Organisational Conflict

Conflict in organisations tends to arise when individuals, groups, teams, departments or even whole organisations are pitted against one another or in some sort of competition with one another. Issues such as differing goals, objectives, reward systems, deadlines and procedural or process differences all have an effect upon potential conflict within organisations.

FOR INSTANCE

Marco worked as a Regional Sales Manager for a Pharmaceutical Company. He's been pretty successful for five years working with his colleagues in the North of England. Recently the company's success had led to the appointment of a second Regional Manager – Sadie – for the North of England thus splitting the Region into two – North of England East and North of England West.

Things started to go wrong right from the outset. It soon became clear that Sadie was hugely competitive and wanted her region to be the best performing in the UK. This would have been OK, as competition can be very healthy for a business. However, Marco discovered that two of Sadie's sales team had been working in his region.

Marco tried to discuss this with Sadie as initially he assumed this was a mistake and would be easily remedied. How wrong he was.

Conflict Styles and Approaches

One of the most frequently quoted theories in relation to approaches for dealing with conflict is the 'Thomas Kilman Conflict Resolution Approach'. This was developed by two American psychologists, K. W. Thomas and R. H. Kilmann who suggest that there are two dimensions of our behaviour that affect the way you deal with conflict:

- **assertiveness** being the extent to which it is necessary for you to satisfy your own concerns
- **co-operation** being the extent to which you attempt to satisfy others' concerns.

These dimensions are then translated in five different approaches to dealing with conflict:

- **avoiding**: neither issue nor person focussed, but more about putting the conflict off for the time being
- **accommodating**: person focussed, where the emphasis is on keeping the peace and not engaging in conflict
- **competing**: issue focussed where you want to win whatever the cost
- **collaborating**: both issue and person focussed where the emphasis is on working together to resolve the conflict
- **compromising**: neither issue nor person focussed, this is about short-term solutions.

You may find it useful to reflect on your approach for dealing with conflict – think about recent conflict situations you have been in and try to identify your default approach. What does this tell you?

We have heard lots of examples from thousands of managers about the different ways people deal with conflict and sadly these are usually negative. We have categorised these into a variety of different 'characters', some of whom you may recognise:

The Emoter. This person is someone who will jump to assumptions and conclusions. An example of this is when someone sends an email full of assumptions and accusations and clearly attacking the recipient. This then engages a response from the recipient and they then react in an emotional way. The result is a defend attack spiral which leads to further conflict and is difficult to resolve.

The Reactor. A person who is the classic poor listener. They don't think things through, have no idea of the effect they are having on others. Never explores meaning, asks questions or probes, just reacts and usually, it's defensively.

The Teller. A person who believes that they are more important than you are. Typically an advocator who always has an opinion and position on all topics, never listens, never probes, never knows whether you might agree with them or not, because you don't get a chance to tell them!

The Bully. A person who is a bit like the teller, but adds a lack of concern and an abuse of power. They will use coercive power to get their own way, threaten and use abusive language. An example of this type of person is a manager who shouts at a junior colleague using abusive language and tells them to shut up. This type of person rarely admits to being a bully and one way of dealing with them is to challenge them or seek advice from others, including Human Resources, to help you plan your strategy.

The Logician. A person who is often unaware of feelings and emotions both their own and others. Their response is cold, logical and does not take account of others' feelings. Will make inappropriate remarks simply because they have no sense of what is appropriate. This type of person thinks everything can be sorted out by applying logic.

The Prevaricator. A person who never faces up to the issue and who sits on the fence. Who avoids the conflict by stalling and evading and hopes that by buying time the conflict will go away. They tend not to like conflict or confrontation.

The Appeaser. A person who focuses on the other person's needs and will tend to give up their own position very quickly. They don't like conflict and will give in to pressure to keep things on an even keel.

None of these ways of dealing with conflict works well, they can make you feel better in the short term but the conflict is rarely solved, simply diverted.

Dealing With Conflict

In order to deal with conflict effectively you need to adopt a structured approach and avoid becoming over emotionally connected with the issue which is the cause of the conflict. We suggest the five-step process in Figure 14.1.

While applying this process you will be using a range of communication, interpersonal and relationship building skills and approaches – listening, questioning, testing understanding, clarifying, summarising, observing, behaviour labelling and feelings commentary.

There are certain other aspects to take into account when dealing with conflict and confrontation. These include:

Dealing With Anger

You will have to deal with both your own anger and that of others. Since we all feel anger at some time or another,

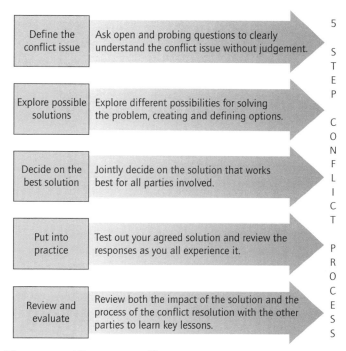

Figure 14.1 Five-step conflict process

it is useful to look at how you deal with your own feelings of anger. One of the first stages in anger management is to identify your anger triggers. What is it that causes you to feel angry? Suppressing anger is not healthy. The most effective way is to control your emotions and learn how to express and channel your anger in an effective way.

Use emotional labelling that indicates to the other person how you are feeling without actually displaying the emotion (i.e. losing your temper). For example you might say something like: 'I am feeling very angry about the way you have ...'. This allows the other person to know how you are feeling without you showing anger. It's about entering into an adult to adult dialogue to explore the issue. This dialogue should involve both parties exploring their perspectives about the situation, actively listening, questioning and observing each other to pick up cues and clues about each other's feelings. The objective is to understand each other's perspectives about the issue, not necessarily to agree with the other person.

> # The objective is to understand each other's perspectives

When anger is displayed by another towards you, your first step is to recognise the other person's feelings. A useful way of disarming anger in another is to immediately recognise it by saying something like – 'I can see that you are angry about this situation, I'd like to understand why. Tell me what it is that is upsetting you?' The key is to recognise the behaviour, name it and explore the issue in order to show the other person that you are genuinely interested in understanding their perspective.

Dealing with Potential Conflict

Skillful leaders and managers are aware of situations where conflict could arise. If you are trying to advocate a position or make a decision then there will naturally be people who do not agree with that position or decision. However, if you think about it in advance and, most importantly, analyse the other stakeholders' positions and feelings before you start discussions, then you will be able to frame your argument in a way that minimises conflict.

Avoiding Conflict

It is impossible to avoid all conflict, but you can and need to, avoid some conflicts. Knowing which conflicts to avoid will help you maintain better relationships at work. It's not always easy to avoid conflict but the key thing is to reflect on the consequences and outcomes of conflict. Don't just get into conflict. Think about it. Think about the other person's position. What's in it for them, what can they gain and what have they got to lose?

Situations where it is wise to avoid getting into conflict with others include:

▌ when you are sure to lose

▌ when winning an argument means losing a relationship

▌ when the topic is meaningless to you (and you are simply arguing a point for the sake of it) but has plenty of meaning for the other person

▌ when winning that battle means losing the war, it is always worth picking your fights.

Apologising and Saying Sorry

If you have managed to get yourself into a conflict which has created an undesirable outcome, and if you feel that the conflict is getting in the way of your effectiveness at work or your relationships at work, what should you do? We see many people who refuse to make the first move. They justify this by saying things like; 'I am right', or 'It's up to them to apologise first.' That is simply foolish pride. We would suggest that you be the one who isn't foolish and ask you to make the first move. An apology doesn't mean you were wrong, it means you have the courage to make a bad situation better. An apology doesn't mean you have to even admit to being wrong. You can say something like 'I apologise if I hurt you, that wasn't my intention', or 'I'm sorry that you felt that I was attacking you, I didn't mean to cause any offence', or 'I'm sorry if I got a bit carried away during that argument, but I tend to get emotional on that topic.'

An apology doesn't mean you were wrong

Apologising first gives the other person the opportunity to reciprocate and to move on. However, you can't use this approach to deal with all conflict situations. The important issue is to be willing to 'eat humble pie' when it is necessary to do so.

IN SUMMARY ...

Here are some top tips for dealing with conflict:

- **Be calm** – above all else, remain calm, unemotional and patient, thus retaining the ability to discuss the issue in a rational and objective way.

- **Show respect** – by acknowledging and demonstrating understanding of the other person's perspective.

- **Seek clarification** – to fully understand the other person's point of view about the issue in question.

- **Listen actively** – to hear what the others have to say and to identify any common interests or agreed perspectives that can be built upon.

- **Develop options** – for possible solutions and explore them with the other parties.

- **Jointly agree a solution or way ahead** – something you can both live with.

- **Reflect and Review** – to learn from the situation.

You have choices. Reflect on the likely consequences and implications of the conflict before getting into it, and above all, master your emotions.

Giving and receiving feedback

The words 'let me give you some feedback', often strike fear into the heart of the receiver. When you hear these words you start to worry about what you have done wrong and what criticism you are going to receive. Instead of looking forward to getting some feedback, you immediately start preparing your defences! This shouldn't be the case. Feedback should always be a way forward, a way of improving your performance and helping you move on. It is quite simply one of the key aspects of managing people and relationships. However, many people find both giving and receiving feedback challenging, difficult, embarrassing and pointless.

Feedback should always be a way forward

So, one of the major challenges you face as an influential leader and manager is giving effective constructive feedback to your reports and colleagues. It seems obvious and easy, but in reality it is one of the hardest tasks to do effectively.

Giving Feedback

Successful feedback depends on both your skill and the quality of the relationship. Honesty and trust are key components.

First, feedback should focus on both the positive and the developmental and never just be given when someone has made a mistake. If the only time you give feedback is when someone has done something wrong then you are sure to develop defensive reactions in your people. Also it is highly unlikely that they make mistakes all of the time. So if you are only seeing what they do wrong, then you need to spend some time catching them doing something right!

Our second point is that before giving your feedback, you need to ask the other person what they think of their own performance. The basic rule is that you must give someone the opportunity to own up to any shortcomings in their performance, before you tell them what you think their shortcomings are! Think about when you do something yourself; you mostly know what you did well and what you could improve. Why should others be any different?

So ask them first, but don't start by asking what they did badly! Ask first what went well, listen attentively and look for points where you agree if you can. Then you can go even further by finding other things that you noticed they did well. Then, and only then, should you ask what they could improve upon or do differently?

Ask first what went well

To recap, this is the procedure to follow:

▌ Ask what they did well or what went well.

▌ Build on their response. You may well have noticed other

things they did well. These can be actions but you can also bring in attitudes. So this might be something like: 'I liked the way you dealt with that customer. In particular, I liked the way you kept calm when they became angry.' Here it is also important to notice even small positive things. You actually have to train yourself to look for positives however small.

▌ Ask what they could improve or do differently.

▌ If they come up with an idea themselves then that is fine, they are more likely to do something about it.

▌ Follow up on their ideas and help them develop their next steps.

Ah, you ask, but what do I do if the other person doesn't see their own mistakes? If they don't see anything to improve, but you do, then continue to resist telling them what they ought to do! Just ask them more specific questions about their performance. For example; 'How do you think the customer felt about that?' or 'How well structured was your presentation?' These specific questions will help the person go back over the situation, and it will also serve as a marker that you feel that there could be an improvement. Again you will need to practise asking good and specific questions here.

If even at this stage they still don't see any problem, then the next step is to challenge. You can do that best by giving the client or participant perspective rather than using negative language. Be clear and firm, but make sure that this is true feedback and not just your subjective perspective. Be careful of the language you use. Avoid accusations and emotional language.

The Managing Director of Performance Consultants Lane 4, and Olympic Gold medallist, Adrian Moorhouse feels that giving feedback skilfully is one of the leader's key tasks. You have to be able to say what you honestly feel about someone's performance, and you have to be able to do it skilfully. He feels that effective delivery of feedback is a great opportunity to improve the relationship between manager and employee. He also is aware that many managers are ineffective when giving and receiving feedback.

Giving feedback skilfully is one of the leader's key tasks

There are certain traps that managers fall into when giving feedback. These include:

- **Being too critical** and giving tough critical feedback to the employee. This leads to defensiveness on the part of the employee and does very little for motivation and morale and rarely contributes to improvements.

- **Applying the notion of constructive feedback**, where the feedback giver will first try to give some positive feedback, then deliver the tough stuff, finally wrapping up with another positive comment, in what the writer and Solution Focused expert Mark McGergow calls 'a nice crunchy feedback sandwich!' The problem with this is it is somewhat formulaic, people see it coming and usually it is simply an attempt to disguise negative feedback.

- **Delivering the feedback clumsily**. In other words there is no praise or recognition of work done well, and the manager has zeroed in only on what is not going well.

- **The manager uses accusatory words**, improper tone or aggressiveness.

FOR INSTANCE

One of our colleagues shared this story with us. One of his former managers once told him 'You are a problem. In fact you have three types of problem! You have a problem with the work you are doing, a problem with your attitude and a problem with authority!

Of course our colleague didn't think he was a problem at all. He was shocked and surprised by what he felt was an unjustified attack on him, and therefore went straight into defensive mode. The feedback was completely valueless.

There are three typical responses to feedback of this type:

- the receiver becomes defensive and no matter what the feedback is will discount it and only hear the negative stuff.
- the receiver does not accept the feedback and no matter how much you point out the positive stuff all they will remember and pay attention to is the bad feedback they hear.
- the feedback receiver becomes demotivated and demoralised, and the net effect will be that at best you have a more challenging relationship in the future, at worst a broken relationship.

In this example it led to a broken relationship and the manager leaving the company for another job.

Some of the key features of good feedback include:

Noticing what is going well, show your appreciation by giving positive feedback regularly – when you notice or experience things going well for and with someone you should always make a point of giving the feedback in the moment. It is far more effective and appreciated to give instant feedback when something has gone well rather than saving it up for monthly meetings or performance reviews.

Being specific – focus on actions, behaviours and giving examples – for instance: 'I particularly liked the way you dealt with that difficult customer. I liked the way you kept your cool and showed respect by listening and questioning them to really understand their complaint.' By adding in the specifics you are really helping people to understand what it is that they actually do well, rather than simply saying 'well done'. The more information you can give them about what has been done well the more it will enable them to incorporate it into their behaviour for next time.

▌ **If appropriate give positive feedback publicly** – if appropriate it is always worth thinking about the value of giving positive feedback publicly. Not only does it then help motivate the person receiving the feedback but others can also learn from the feedback. So, for example, if one of your team has just won a large piece of business then you may like to thank them at the next team meeting, and perhaps ask them if there are any lessons to be learned from the experience which they can then share with the others. A nice addition to this is to show your appreciation with both words of praise and a bunch of flowers or bottle of champagne or similar! Of course this should not be overdone as it can then lose the effect.

▌ **Constructive feedback or developmental feedback should always be given in private** – never criticise someone in public, it is a sure way of destroying a relationship. When you have developmental (or negative) feedback to give, it's important to get the timing right and offer the feedback as soon as possible after the event while both memories are still clear.

▌ **Always give the feedback recipient the opportunity to respond and ask questions to ensure understanding** – sometimes feedback givers forget this bit as they are so keen to give the feedback and move on. They forget that half the battle is to make sure the feedback is understood and taken on board. So give the feedback, then enter into a dialogue to ensure understanding, and to agree on how the feedback will be used in future.

▌ **Adopting a positive focus** – even when dealing with the negative. It is important that feedback is seen as a positive process. So, when giving constructive criticism it is important to focus on what positives can emerge from the experience. If you adopt a learning perspective and help the person to see how they can improve then even negative feedback can have a positive effect.

People like to be recognised and appreciated for good work, and equally they appreciate having good quality feedback and support when things are not going so well, so that they can develop their skills for the future. Good quality feedback leads to a more motivated and engaged team, and managers who have mastered the skill of feedback demonstrate good relationship management by showing real interest in the other person.

Receiving Feedback

Giving feedback is only half the story. Receiving feedback and actually encouraging a feedback climate in your team, department or organisation is the key to true success in this area.

Modelling the feedback process by asking for and acting on feedback about yourself involves:

▌ **Recognising what it is you want to develop and therefore get feedback on** – relationally skilled leaders and managers are curious about the impact they have on others and the effect their behaviour has in different situations. They tend to be self-aware, so have a good understanding of their strengths and weaknesses. These are all areas where feedback from others will be useful to help you grow and develop even further.

▌ **Asking open questions of others about your behaviour and performance** – this is the easiest way of getting feedback. However it is best to be very specific about the questions you ask. So, rather than say something like

'How effective was I at chairing that meeting?' where the response will often be very generalised such as; 'Fine', or 'You could have brought more people in', or 'You could have stuck more to the agenda'. While this may be useful, you may really want information about your body language during the meeting. So, construct your question accordingly, so that you get feedback focussed on this area. For example: ask 'I'd like some feedback about my body language during that last team meeting. Can you tell me how you think it affected the process? What exactly did I do that helped and what hindered?' This is far more specific and will give you better quality feedback to work on in future meetings.

▌ **Identifying people you trust to observe your behaviour and give you feedback** – it is always best to ask people you trust to observe and give you feedback. Indeed, if you identify a range of people who fall into this category, you can pre-brief them when you are working with them to observe your behaviour in different situations. They can then give you feedback on specific aspects of your behaviour and skills.

▌ **Accepting the feedback without becoming defensive** – this is the difficult bit. It is very easy to get the feedback then go into defence mode and offer excuses as to why you do something. It is far better to enter a dialogue to establish full understanding about the feedback, accept it, explore with the feedback giver what might be more effective, or how you can be even more effective. You should frame the feedback not as criticism but as an opportunity to improve your skills and performance. This, of course, depends to a great extent on the skill of the feedback giver.

Developing a feedback culture

There are many different ways of developing a feedback culture in your business. It's not easy; it takes time, effort and practice but will pay dividends in the end. Here are some ideas:

▊ **Performance Review**. Most of you will undoubtedly have a performance review discussion with your boss and your reports at least once a year, this is a real opportunity to both give and receive feedback during these discussions (when you are with your boss and when you are reviewing others). During your performance review discussions with your team don't just practise your feedback giving technique. It is a great opportunity to begin building in opportunities to receive feedback as well. So, why not ask questions like:

▊ What can I do that could help you be even more effective in your job?

▊ What do I do that prevents you performing to your best?

▊ How do you like to be managed?

▊ What support do you need from me?

▊ **Training Programmes and Psychometrics** – management development programmes are a frequent feature of contemporary organisational life. During development programmes there are many opportunities to practise your feedback skills and to ask others for feedback. During any experiential session you will often find yourself in situations where formal feedback processes are instituted by the trainers. This is good practice and development for both giving and receiving feedback. However, in addition to the formal part you could ask some of your fellow participants for feedback about your contribution during these sessions.

Psychometrics also feature on a regular basis in many management development programmes and these provide a prime opportunity to identify areas for you to explore with others. Once identified you can then decide which areas are of most importance to your current job and future development and you can then ask appropriate colleagues for feedback. For example, try to get some psychometric questionnaires done for you and your team. They are a good catalyst for open discussion.

▌ **Review processes** – there are a variety of processes that you can easily introduce to your daily work life that will encourage a feedback culture. These include:

▌ At the end of team meetings, encourage feedback by asking everyone to say something they enjoyed/found useful/want to do more of about the meeting. Once the team have become used to doing this, you could add to the process by encouraging them to say something they'd like to develop or do differently

▌ Again during team meetings ask your colleagues to turn to the person sitting on their left (or right which ever you prefer) and give that person feedback about something you appreciate about working with them

▌ Give everyone a sheet of paper and ask them to write down what they thought went well and what they think could be done even better. Then, collectively share views and examine the patterns that emerge. Agree how to implement any appropriate changes based on the feedback.

IN SUMMARY …

We find these two simple mnemonics' to be very effective reminders of what feedback should be and shouldn't be.

Remember Feedback should **BOOST**	Should not be **BORING**
B alanced	B iased
O bserved	O ver the top
O wned	R epetitive
S pecific	I nsensitive
T imely	N egative
	G oading

16
Managing challenge

When engaging with others, effective leaders and managers recognise that there are two aspects of challenge to consider. The first is your ability to challenge others skilfully and effectively, and the second is your ability to deal with people who challenge you. To be successful you need to develop capability in both scenarios. Effective leaders recognise that developing high quality relationships demands the ability to have robust conversations with others where mutual challenge is a feature. The presence of challenge in discussion means that all parties are able to reach greater breadth and depth in debate, and consequently better outcomes may emerge.

You as Challenger

As a challenger, there are many different situations where you have to challenge others. However, we have found that the following three areas are those that challenge managers the most

▌ when you disagree with someone

▌ when you have to challenge poor performance

▌ when you need to test out what people are capable of.

When you disagree with something or someone

As a leader or manager you are in a responsible position, and it is your duty to speak up if you see something that you disagree with, or that you think is not right. It's no use disagreeing with something and just shaking your head and doing nothing about it, or worse, grumbling behind people's backs. We find that many leaders and managers are unable to challenge effectively. When they challenge it tends to be in a blunt and robust way, often creating more problems than it solves. The idea is not just to disagree, or criticise the other person or their ideas, but rather to speak up, voice your concern and express it in a challenging, yet positive way.

It is your duty to speak up if you see something you disagree with

For example, if you disagree with a colleague's opinion on something, don't just say, 'I disagree', or 'That won't work!' It will be far more effective to start by looking for something in your colleague's opinion that you can agree with. After all it is unlikely that they are talking 100 per cent nonsense. It is far more effective to say something like – 'I like your focus on the financial aspects of the situation, however, I'm not sure about the specifics.' Or, 'That's an interesting strategic perspective and I'm not sure I agree with all the details, can we look at things in a bit more depth?'

Remember, when you disagree you still have to work together to reach an understanding.

Challenging poor performance

A common mistake managers make when addressing issues of performance is that they confuse the issue and the person. If you label someone as a poor performer or as a problem, it might help you get your feelings off your chest, but it won't help solve the issue.

Remember, while it's acceptable to challenge, it should be directed at the behaviour and not the person. Too often, managers make their challenge directly about the person, rather than about the behaviour. Try to focus on the issue or problem rather than simply criticising the person. Direct criticism of the person won't get the results you want; it will simply create resentment and anger. It is much better to talk about behaviours and to point out what behaviours you would prefer to see. Be specific and give others help and support to achieve the change. If there is a competence issue, then offer the training and support they need. If it's a question of motivation, start by finding out what really motivates them.

The best way to do this is to take the time to ask them and to listen carefully. Then you will have the necessary knowledge and information to be able to make links between the achievement of the tasks and motivation. One example is if someone is motivated by recognition, then you can find a way to give them more recognition when they achieve goals successfully. Or, if their motivation is autonomy, then you can look for ways to give them a bit more autonomy, while making it clear that this is on the understanding the task is completed to your satisfaction.

If it's a question of negative attitude (i.e. a 'won't do' attitude) it's slightly more complex. Rather than immediately jumping to challenge, you might start by pointing out the negative implications of that behaviour (in a calm way) and then explore possible alternatives with the person.

So, instead of immediately reacting to the provocation, we are asking you to remain calm, point out some of the negative implications of the behaviour, and then look at different options. One of these options might be to simply ask the person why they don't feel it's part of their job. You would then be in a discussion about the job rather than in an argument. The last thing you want in your organisation is a sullen, unco-operative person. They do exist, but don't assume that is the problem. They may well be sullen and unco-operative because of you!

FOR INSTANCE

A colleague refuses to do something you think is part of their job. You might become irritated and frustrated and start threatening them. They would, in all probability, become defensive or aggressive, and thus the situation would deteriorate into a negative attack defence spiral. You had an unco-operative person, now you have a negative, angry and defensive unco-operative person!

Challenging lack of confidence

Challenging is not just about being critical and disagreeing with someone. It can also be about stretching people, getting them to do something you believe they can do, but they don't believe they can do it. Often this can be due to lack of confidence or possibly lack of self belief. As an influential leader it is your responsibility to be aware of people's potential and helps them realise that potential.

> It is your responsibility to be aware of people's potential

FOR INSTANCE

Our late colleague, Robert MacGregor, was famous for his challenges which encouraged others to push the boundaries and enabled them to learn and grow. On one occasion he phoned his assistant to tell her he was going to be delayed for an after dinner speech with a group of participants. He asked her if she would get things going by starting the session off. Karen was of course extremely nervous, but felt there was no option but to go ahead. She ended up chairing the whole evening extremely successfully, as Bob knew she would!

Bob believed in her ability and potential, and he knew she had the capability to succeed; she just needed a little push, and the opportunity. He also knew Karen sufficiently well and knew that she would not let him down and therefore his challenge in this case was appropriate. Had he simply asked Karen to chair the evening she would have in all likelihood declined, because she didn't feel competent. During all of this, Bob wasn't stuck in traffic in his car as claimed, but sipping a pint in the Ashridge bar a few yards away! This is of course a risky strategy and only appropriate in those circumstances when you know you are on safe ground and are certain the person can cope with the challenge.

The key point about challenging to develop potential is to be sure of the person's capability, and to recognise that the barrier to their realising that potential is an inner one – lack of confidence, and not lack of ability.

To illustrate this effective use of challenge to develop potential and to overcome lack of confidence, here's a story involving Mike and his lack of belief in his ability to fly a plane.

FOR INSTANCE

One of Mike's clients, Paul, is a flight instructor in his spare time. After one of their business meetings he offered Mike a flight in his small plane. Arriving at the airport he showed Mike around the plane, checking all the things that needed to be checked, then sat him in the pilot's seat and explained all the instruments. Then Paul casually asked Mike to steer the plane onto the runway. He managed to do that and when the plane was sitting at the end of the runway, Mike was expecting Paul to assume control and take off. To Mike's horror Paul instructed him to open up the throttle a little and keep the plane on the central painted line on the runway. As Mike focussed on doing that Paul asked him to open the throttle a bit more then pull up on the joystick...! Before Mike knew what was happening he was flying the plane.

This completely unexpected challenge helped Mike to overcome all the barriers he would certainly have put up.

Now if he had asked Mike to do a take off and fly a plane without any previous experience he would have run a mile. So that was a very real challenge, but done in a skilful and positive way. Of course, the plane had dual controls and he could have taken control at any moment. If it had been a plane with single controls then the challenge would have been unskilful, overdone and plain dangerous.

Your challenge should be appropriate. Remember it is designed to improve someone's performance not to demotivate and demoralise! Try to frame your challenge positively rather than negatively. For example, if you feel someone is capable of doing something, then tell them why. Help them to focus on their skills, talents and energy rather than focusing on what they can't do or didn't do. As our 'For instances' demonstrate, challenges can be broken down into smaller more attainable chunks.

For those of you who are already committed challengers, your job is to manage challenge effectively. The key is to challenge in a positive way, rather than sniping, complaining and gossiping. For those of you who see a better way of doing things, but don't say or do anything, your task is to take your courage in both hands, and dare to challenge. The point is that challenge is not done just for the sake

Your job is to manage challenge effectively

of challenge, but to improve people's performance and ultimately the way the organisation works.

It is important to ensure that the motivation for challenge is well intentioned and that the person being challenged has a good chance of coping with the challenge. If one or both of these are missing then you are not challenging, you are bullying!

Skills for Effective Challengers

Some things you can do:

▌ **Make sure you really understand your organisation's culture, both formal and informal**. Get to know the accepted practices and the unwritten informal rules. This is especially true when you join a new organisation. It can take time to get to know a new organisation and that time will be well spent. You may have great ideas, suggestions and perspectives about your new organisation, but if you start off by challenging things that have been in existence for several years, you may be seen as arrogant. Unless you have been specifically asked for your advice, try to hold back from going in and giving advice prematurely. Many people have great ideas but get the timing and manner of their challenge wrong. Work with the culture rather than against it. If you can learn to challenge 'with the grain', rather than against it, your challenge will be all the more effective. This also applies if you are working in an international environment. Get to know the local culture and adapt your challenge style to it. Some countries will not accept the type of direct challenge that a British or American manager, for example, would use.

FOR INSTANCE

We were working in China with a group of managers from the company's Asia Pacific region. One of the managers was an American expatriate who had arrived fairly recently in China. He disagreed with some of the actions and decisions taken by the team and disagreed loudly and directly with the team leader in public. The other managers were taken aback by this blunt challenge. We knew that some of them actually agreed with their American colleague in private, but didn't dare to challenge their boss directly and in public. The American manager didn't do himself any favours by this action. He needed to learn that you don't directly challenge your boss in that culture.

Build networks and relations within the organisation. Although you may disagree with the ways things are, you can still build networks and positive relationships. If you don't take the time and trouble to build and maintain relationships you will find yourself isolated and without support when things get tough.

FOR INSTANCE

One manager we know spent so much time and energy focusing on the tasks given to him by his CEO that he ignored his colleagues and direct reports with whom he had previously had good relationships. As time went on and the pressure of work became more intense for him, he found himself falling out with colleagues, and getting into arguments with them. He soon found himself isolated from them. Then he gradually lost the support of his direct reports because he was too busy to spend time with them. He was working 12 to 14 hour days and was under intense pressure. He became aggressive and short tempered, failed to engage with others, and ignored the needs of his people. The end result was that he was forced out of the organisation on the grounds that he wasn't doing his job as a manager effectively! Unfair perhaps, but it shows the danger of focussing exclusively on the task to the detriment of people and relationships.

▌ **Do not define your work life by the fact that you always challenge others** – it would be an exceptional organisation where you agreed or disagreed with everything. The influential leader and manager chooses the issues to focus on. Do not moan and complain about everything, otherwise you'll soon find yourself in no man's land. As the saying goes, it's no use winning the battle and losing the war. It's a common phrase but a true one, choose your battles wisely!

▌ **Focus on the positive not negative.** Rather than focusing on what you don't like, try looking at the positive aspects of a situation. Propose solutions rather than just moaning. Nothing is more likely to turn people against you than if you constantly whinge about what's wrong, but have no positive solutions to offer. Force yourself to think of possible solutions to a problem before you complain or challenge. That way you will have something worthwhile to offer.

▌ **Talk to someone first.** Talking issues over with others can often help. In fact, if you were thinking of challenging someone, or the way things are being done, confiding your plans to a trusted colleague would be an excellent idea! They can let you know if your challenge is framed in the right way, and how it will be perceived. We think you should actively look for a colleague to do this or find a mentor within your organisation to help you in these cases.

Managing Challengers

There are a range of different types of challengers within an organisation. They range from people who occasionally disagree with something you do or say, to the inveterate challengers who, by nature, like to challenge everything and everyone. There are also many types of challenge, and both challenge and challengers can be constructive or not.

Your task is to manage these situations effectively. The challenger also has to manage their behaviour effectively. If organisations are to be effective in adapting to change, their managers must be able to both challenge others, and handle challenge themselves. They must accept that they cannot control everything and everyone, rather they must champion the challenger, learn to accept that those who challenge are usually trying to help the organisation, even though their methods may be different.

Champion the challenger

FOR INSTANCE

Adrian Moorhouse, MD of Lane 4, thinks that everyone in his company has to be able to say what they feel. They must be free to say what is on their mind rather than just keeping silent. He also points out that leaders need to be able to challenge themselves and to give up control to others and not keep all the decisions for themselves. Not an easy task when you are the boss and people are looking to you for the answers.

Managing challengers is about encouraging diversity and creativity. It is about getting your colleagues to offer different perspectives, be more creative and more involved. It is about giving up control and losing the 'if you're not with us you're against us' mentality that characterises many organisations. It isn't easy to manage challenge. Those who challenge may be viewed as mavericks and rebels and have a fairly negative reputation. However, as we have discussed, challenge can be a source of value to the organisation, so learning how to deal with challenge should be seen as an integral part of the manager's job.

Here are some guidelines ...

▌ **Don't just recruit people to your team or organisation who are the same as the people you already have**. Research shows us that when recruiting people, recruiters often prefer people who are similar to themselves. Coupled with the fact that the selection process is often weighed against non-conformists, we end up bringing in people who share the same view of the world as the organisation. This clearly limits challenge. We are not arguing for a process that employs only radically different people, but there has to be a process in selection which allows for people who do not necessarily fit the existing mould. The advantages of this are that there are likely to be more creative ideas within the organisation, the status quo can be challenged, the unsayable can be said, and previously suppressed issues can be raised.

▌ **Try to encourage challenge in your own departments**. If, as is likely, you already have challengers in the organisation, rather than forcing them to agree, why not try encouraging their ideas, and empowering them to do something about it? So, the next time one of your colleagues challenges your ideas, instead of blocking them or disagreeing with them, encourage them to think more about the issue and to do some research into their perspective. This empowers them and gives their challenge a focus.

▌ **Accept existing challenge**. If everyone in your team agrees with you, you're wasting a lot of money on their salaries. If all you need are people to agree with you and execute your orders, then you don't need highly educated and well paid team members. Robots will obey more easily!

▌ **Accept that challenge doesn't always mean disagreement**. So when you are challenged by someone, rather than automatically disagreeing or rejecting, stop for a moment, reflect and ask open questions to understand where the challenger is coming from. This often leads to greater innovation and creativity where two heads are better than one.

So, learning how to challenge effectively, but also learning how to encourage and accept challenge by others are both skills that the effective leader masters.

IN SUMMARY ...

Here are some tips for managing challenge and challengers:

- Be open to challenge.
- Encourage challenge, be proactive and ask for others' thoughts.
- Nominate a devil's advocate.
- Help challengers to have a say.
- Help challengers frame their challenges in a positive and constructive way.
- Encourage challengers to actually do something and not just criticise.
- Create an open environment where people are not afraid to challenge you.

How to be appreciative

Being appreciative and showing positive appreciation to your people might not come naturally to all leaders. As one leader said, 'It sounds kind of pink and fluffy to me!' And that is a fairly typical response when we introduce managers to the concept of being appreciative.

We know, however, that showing appreciation to others is a fundamental aspect of successful influencing and effective relationships. The need to be valued and appreciated is a fundamental human one, and if you are to engage successfully with others to get effective performance, then you need to be able to grasp the basic psychology of appreciation.

The need to be appreciated is a fundamental human one

Traditionally, leaders use what we might call a deficit model when dealing with situations at work. That is to say you assume that things are a problem and that you need to fix the problem. So you focus on what is going wrong and what is not working!

FOR INSTANCE

Mike spent a couple of years in the 1980s as a management consultant going into companies in order to help them become more effective. His job was to reduce costs in the organisation – and he was told to go in, investigate and come back with savings of around 30 per sent. Back then it wasn't always that difficult to achieve such cost reductions, but sometimes he would go into a department which was run effectively and he couldn't find that 30 per cent – only perhaps 10 per cent.

But his manager would tell him to go back and stay there until he found the other 20 per cent. The basic assumption was that the department was not run properly and that we needed to fix the problem. There was no focus on finding out what worked well and building on it, just a focus on the problems that needed to be found then fixed. Needless to say this approach didn't do too much for the morale of the organisation or people concerned – nor Mike for that matter.

This approach is not just limited to business. In the field of psychology there has been a focus on what is wrong with a person and what is not going well. It tends to look at fixing a person's problems and correcting weaknesses. Nowadays the idea that psychology should be equally interested in what is going well is gaining ground. If someone is holding down a regular position within an organisation they must be doing something right.

Often a person's situation is not completely negative, but we just have a tendency to focus in on what is not going well, rather than stepping back and trying to think about what is actually going well. We tend to zoom into the problems and let them fill all the space in our mind.

How does this apply to relations at work and effective influencing? Well often if you have a problem with someone, you tend to amplify the problem and apply it to everything you do. The other person becomes a 'problem' person. Many of the managers we work with come to us asking for help in dealing with problem people. But what if the other person was not a problem? After all they probably don't describe themselves as a problem person! And what does it do to the relationship between you and the other person if you are already labelling them as a problem? How would you feel if your boss was describing you as a problem?

Relationally intelligent leaders would do two things:

▌ **They would focus on the relationship and not just the person**. They would have the courage to realise that they are part of the 'problem' too. They would think about how they might be contributing to the issue, and focusing on what *they* could try to do differently. As the saying goes, 'If you always do what you always did you'll always get what you always got' So try doing something different yourself!

▌ **They would also look for some positives about the other person or persons involved**. Are they *always* a problem? When are they not a problem? What have they done well in the past? What are they doing right now that is not a problem? What are they doing well?

Once you have established that the person is not all bad and useless, you can start to build on that more positive platform and arrive at much more effective outcomes.

FOR INSTANCE

Hans is the CEO of a small manufacturing company. He has a fraught relationship with his personal assistant who he finds fussy, annoying and exasperating. The relationship has become progressively worse over a period of time which led to the PA becoming unproductive. Hans's way of dealing with this was to focus on all the things that annoyed him and unsurprisingly this led to an even worse situation to the extent that the relationship was really beginning to break down.

Hans discussed this issue with us and we suggested that he try taking an appreciative approach rather than focussing on the negative. We helped Hans to develop a plan of action. This involved getting Hans to identify the positive aspects of her performance which he had previously ignored. Following a period of time where Hans applied this process he found that his PA became much more motivated, did more of what she already did well and became more receptive to developing her weaker areas. On the whole their relationship has improved dramatically and has become significantly more productive.

Hans has told us that this experience has taught him that you can turn round a difficult relationship and that appreciative principles actually do work.

Let's face it, you are not going to make things better by focussing on what a person does badly. You are not going to get them in a positive frame of mind to do something about the so-called problem by being negative and critical of them. They are just going to feel resentful. Whether they are at fault or not is pretty much irrelevant. The fact is you are the leader or manager and you need to become really skilled at showing appreciation, focussing on strengths and solutions, so that you start to get the outcome and results you want. You certainly will not get effective outcomes by getting angry and critical. You need to be much more nuanced and skilful.

Psychologists believe that a great deal of appreciative emotion is essential for creativity and for building effective relationships and networks. We also believe that these are key areas for successful organisations. The idea is that human beings are drawn towards the positive and away

You need to be nuanced and skilful

from the negative. So if you are able to focus more on the positives than the negatives in a person, you will actually be a more effective leader.

There is another aspect of this theory too. It is that our moods and behaviours are more affected by the negative than by the positive. So for example, although people will be happy to receive praise, any criticism will have a greater and longer lasting impact on them. You will remember the criticism far more than any praise you are given. So you might unwittingly criticise someone and think nothing of it, but that will affect their behaviour and attitude towards you for a long time. In order to redress the balance you need to give a higher amount of positive feedback.

In fact, according to research by Professor Marcial Losada, the ratio of positive to negative should be almost three to one. He looked at 60 business organisations and measured their effectiveness in terms of profitability, customer satisfaction and employee attitudes. And he found that for organisations to be effective, leaders needed to do two things.

- **Inquire more than you advocate**. That means that you need to be asking more questions and doing more listening rather than simply telling people what to do.

- **Be more appreciative than negative in your interactions**. For really effective teams the ratio of positivity to negativity was five to one! Just think about it for a moment: five to one! You need to be giving five times as much positive feedback as negative feedback. How close is your ratio to that?

So the question you need to ask yourself is, what is the ratio of positivity to negativity in your interactions? How much do you actually ask questions and listen to others, rather than simply putting forward your thoughts and opinions?

Interestingly, a ratio of one to one is not considered sufficient to make a difference. In fact many of you might think that you don't even receive that much, and that you are actually getting more negative comments and feedback than positive ones. So perhaps aiming for a one to one ratio might be a start, but three to one (or higher) should be your goal!

Being more appreciative also leads to being more altruistic, more curious, more creative and more open to learning. These are all attributes of an effective leader.

How to respond constructively to others

Building and maintaining effective relationships not only means being positive and appreciative when things are going badly. How we respond to others' good news also affects our relationships. So, for example, if someone comes to you and tells you a piece of good news, let's say a promotion, you can respond in four basic ways. According to Professor Shelly Gable of the University of California you can respond either actively or passively, and you can be either constructive or destructive.

Let's look at the possible ways you can respond to others. In this example a colleague has come to tell you about a promotion they have just received.

Passive constructive. Clearly you would want to react in a constructive way, but even then you can often be quite passive. So you might say something like 'Well done!' then move quickly onto another subject. This clearly shows that you are not that interested in what the other person has to say.

Active destructive. An even worse way to respond would be to have a destructive approach. This could be active or passive. So an active, but destructive response would be to focus on the negatives and say something like 'Oh that's a lot of work to take on! Are you sure you're ready for it?'

Passive destructive. A passive destructive response would be just to move on to a completely different subject without even acknowledging the promotion! You can imagine the negative effect on your relationship.

Active constructive. What we would suggest is that you use the 'active constructive' approach. So in this example you could say something like, 'That's excellent news. I know it means a lot to you!' You would then ask some open questions about the job, or the person's feelings, or their plans for the new job. Or all of these! This then demonstrates clear interest in the other, builds and strengthens your relationships and has the added benefit of contributing towards your leadership effectiveness!

In case you are wondering if it's ever appropriate to be negative and pessimistic, then let us reassure you! The theory of positive psychology tells us that you should not usually go over a ratio of ten positive to one negative. That would be considered unrealistically positive and therefore may come across as false. It also tells us that your optimism should be flexible and that you need to be realistically pessimistic. In other words, you can be pessimistic or negative when the costs of failure are high or when talking to a person whose prospects are not good. In these cases you should not be unduly optimistic but rather more realistic.

You need to be realistically pessimistic

Positive Affirmation

Positive affirmation is a technique used to give systematic positive feedback to others. For example, when you are working with a person you would actively look for something that they do well and share that positive feedback with them there and then. You start focussing your attention on what people do well rather than what they are lacking.

The concept of positive affirmation is commonly used during training workshops. Typically you are asked to say something positive and affirmative to each of your fellow participants. At first people tend to find this extremely difficult. What to say? How to say it without sounding false? But after a slow start most people are able to notice and appreciate many things about others, things that you probably would not have previously noticed. As people become more skilled at giving positive affirmations it becomes more natural.

The point of making positive affirmations is twofold:

▎ you encourage and motivate the other person by noticing and saying what they have done well

▎ you start focussing your attention on what people do well rather than what they are lacking.

FOR INSTANCE

We use a version of positive affirmations on one of our workshops at Ashridge. We put all the participants' names up on a wall chart and then ask everyone to write down something positive about all the other participants throughout the three days. We hand out Post It notes and ask them to stick them up on the board. Naturally it's a bit slow to start with, but things start moving along as people take notice of what others are doing well, or are bringing to the sessions. Of course not everything is positive but we don't allow them to write down anything negative – just ask them to focus on the positives. What then happens is that at the end of the seminar everybody collects their positive affirmations, reads them and then takes them home in an envelope.

We find that three things happen. One is that our participants really start to become more aware of others, and notice much more than they did previously. Additionally, they also start to become aware of their own positive contributions and third, their energy level and confidence increases dramatically.

The other thing to remember is that it costs you absolutely nothing to do this. It's free! All it takes is a bit of attention to others, a positive perspective and the ability to appreciate rather than criticise.

EXERCISE

Write down three things you are good at – at work.

Then ask yourself, what else do I do well at work? Then ask yourself what else? What else? And what else? Keep on asking until you have at least 20 things written down.

Look at the list. How does that make you feel? How easy was it? If you found this exercise a little bit difficult then we have just shown that you tend to find it hard to focus on positives rather than negatives! Would it have been easier if we had asked you to write down things you were bad at?

You can use this exercise with your team as well.

IN SUMMARY ...

To develop and demonstrate you skills and abilities in this area you should:

- Start noticing small things that people are doing well and compliment them on them.
- Start to say the positive and appreciative things you notice about others to your colleagues.
- Think about your own behaviour and the balance of positive versus negative.
- Set yourself a challenge to say at least three positive and appreciative pieces of feedback every day, you soon won't have to set the challenge as you will notice the difference and do it automatically.

Reframing 18

There is nothing good or bad but thinking makes it so

William Shakespeare, Hamlet Act 2, scene 2

Reframing is a key tool for successful communication. Influential and relationally aware leaders and managers recognise the importance of developing their skill and expertise in this area. The effective use of reframing is an important aspect of helping both you and others to see things from a different, more useful perspective.

What do we mean by reframing?

Reframing is when you change the context or perspective of how a situation is viewed, with the intent of enabling people to view that situation in a more useful and productive way. It's about changing how you and others look at the situation, by viewing the situation from a different perspective. This new perspective must of course still fit the facts of the situation but allows a different interpretation.

> View the situation from a different perspective

FOR INSTANCE

Let's take a simple yet real example to illustrate. You are attending a business seminar abroad, which ends earlier than expected. You have booked a late flight and when you find out that the meeting will finish earlier than expected, you naturally try to rebook on an earlier flight so you can be home at a reasonable time. Unfortunately the airline cannot rebook your ticket. So you become angry and frustrated. You will have a wasted afternoon and get home late. You spend the afternoon hanging around unproductively and venting your anger on your organisation, your boss, the airline, and even yourself for not clarifying the finishing time.

Or do you?

Perhaps you are able to see this as an opportunity? After all the conference centre has an excellent library and resource centre. Perhaps this is a good opportunity to thumb through a few books and articles on the subject of leadership? There's also the gym, you could get a bit of extra exercise. Perhaps you could read for an hour or so, then have a session in the gym then go for a walk in the beautiful park near the office. You don't often get a chance to read and relax in your busy schedule. Then you would arrive in plenty of time at the airport and arrive home relaxed, unstressed and in an excellent mood to face the weekend. If you try to see this delay as an unexpected opportunity, then you have been able to reframe the experience – and turn it from a negative experience into a positive opportunity.

Reframing is all about managing meaning. The effective mastery of reframing gives you the choice to see the same situation in different ways. More importantly it gives you the ability to help others see situations in different, more productive, ways.

Reframing is about managing meaning

Effective Reframing is a skill that allows others and yourself to accept one interpretation of a situation or event, over another. But the different interpretation must make sense to the other person and not just the person doing the reframing. The reframe must therefore have meaning for the other person. In essence, to frame and reframe is to choose one meaning or interpretation of an event over another.

Frames determine whether people notice problems, how they understand them and how they evaluate and act on them. So, as an effective leader, you need to have the flexibility to frame issues from several different perspectives, and then choose the most appropriate frame for the situation. As Richard Bandler and John Grinder, founders of neuro linguistic programming (NLP) said 'As a communicator you want to have the ability to shift the frames that people put around anything'.

Organisations have found reframing to be a useful tool for influencing stakeholders.

FOR INSTANCE

In the 1990s a US car firm was in trouble and needed to convince the US Congress to give them money to help them out. Normally it's not the job of US Congress to bail out private firms, but their CEO reminded Congress that the company was the 10th largest in the USA, and employed some 600,000 people. He then framed the problem as America's problem and not just the company's problem. Having effectively reframed the situation the CEO was able to persuade the US government to give them the money.

More recently the new CEO of this company had to go back to the US government to ask for money to bail them out again. This time they were not so smart – their CEO took a private jet to Washington to ask the Congress for money. It's particularly hard to frame your company as being bankrupt when you can still afford a private jet!

Reframing is an absolute necessity for effective communicators. It helps others to 'see' differently, and is an essential part of the effective leader's and influencer's toolkit.

We use framing as a way of helping people understand things in a more positive and resourceful way. However, there can be disadvantages to Framing and Reframing if they are done in a cynical way. For example, some companies frame their organisation as a family or talk about how people are their most important asset. This has advantages of course: you might feel more attached to the company and be more motivated with a sense of belonging. You would be more likely to do favours for others without seeking monetary reward, and perhaps have a greater sense of trust.

But there are also clear disadvantages; when bad times come and the company wants to downsize and get rid of your job, it suddenly starts looking a lot less like a family. For the people who were made redundant, the 'family/important people' frame clearly was not a true frame. Further and possibly even more dangerously, for those who remain in the company the 'Family/important people' frame will no longer have any meaning. And any further attempt by management to influence using this frame will be looked on with distrust and cynicism.

The clear message is, make sure you are not framing and reframing as a tool to manipulate people.

Different Types of Framing and Reframing

Let's explore the different types of frame and reframe:

Framing and behaviour

The way you act towards a person or a situation depends on how you frame that person or situation. For example, if you frame someone as a problem performer (which we often hear in our work with people in organisations) and focus only on when they are being a problem, you will not be able to see anything other than problems. So it is helpful then to ask yourself some specific questions about this person in order to identify when they are not being a problem. In other words, you are reframing the situation from negative to positive. You can try to focus on times when they have demonstrated ambition or initiative. You can actively look for times when they have been helpful or have been successful. When they have perhaps shown creativity or support?

Of course if you know them well you probably know enough about them to start reframing immediately. But if you do not then you can be even more skilful and add another tool, inquiry, to your repertoire. So you could then ask some probing questions by inquiring into the details of their job, asking specific questions about what they enjoy, what they are good at, asking when they were at their best, when and where they could do even better and start helping them to focus on some specific steps forward.

The idea is to stop framing the person as a problem and start to look at more positive frames. You can focus on when they are not being a problem, which is more useful. No person is a problem all of the time. However, it's very easy to start defining people as problems, but the act of defining or framing them, as a problem, will certainly not help you to achieve a positive outcome!

Start to look at more positive frames

Reframing the past

Often you look negatively at what you did in the past, and this can affect your abilities and motivation in the present and in the future. It can be useful sometimes to reframe the past, especially if the frame you used was too negative or harsh. Obviously, it would not be useful if you were to distort the past and to deny reality would be self-defeating. But if your view of the past prevents you from doing things in the present, it can be useful to go back and reframe what happened.

For example, you might think of yourself as lacking the confidence and ability to speak in public because of the disastrous speech you made at school when you were much younger. You have framed this event as a disaster and a failure, and it is still affecting your ability to do things now. Looking back you could now reframe that event as one that showed courage. Giving a speech to a large audience at any age is a challenge, and while it didn't go too well you certainly learned a lot. Instead of a purely negative frame, you can reframe the past in a more positive, but still real, way.

Framing vision

Many leaders have a vision of where they want their organisation to be in the future. Although this is generally a good idea, it is important to ensure that the vision is clearly linked to the real hopes and aspirations of the people in the organisation. You need to make sure that your vision is also framed from their perspective. You need to understand the context and the values of the people who are going to make your vision a reality, and link your vision to theirs.

Going back to our US car company story; when their leaders flew to Washington in 2009 to ask for government money, they flew in a private jet! That specific action is a frame, a frame which tells everyone that the leaders are more important than others in the company, and a frame which could have been interpreted by the US government as showing that the company's leaders were disconnected from reality. Travelling to Washington by car, one of their own cars of course, would have been a much more effective way.

Reframing blame

We find that people often tend to be critical and start to blame themselves or others if something goes wrong. But is this useful? What purpose does the blame serve? Blame is a useless emotion which elicits judgemental language and tones and leads to defensiveness. It is far better to reframe and focus instead on the desirable outcomes from a situation. By turning your attention to what you *can* do or what others can do, rather than dwelling on what you and they cannot do, you have reframed blame into a more positive emotion.

What purpose does blame serve?

Reframing failure

Many people think of an event where they did not get what they wanted as 'failure'. Rather than framing it in that way, it is much more effective to think of it as excellent feedback. By all means look at what you didn't do well, but rather than blaming yourself (which is totally unproductive) try to learn from the event. Focus on what you learned and what you could do differently and you will find that you are in a better, more resourceful state to learn and progress.

Reframing assumptions

Often we make assumptions about people and situations. Assumptions can be very dangerous and negative. It's a very lazy habit to get into and one you can avoid by simply being curious. So instead of assuming things you simply need to ask questions, explore more and find out what is an assumption on your part and what is reality.

Reframing for influence

How do you use reframing in an influencing context?

Usually, when you are trying to influence someone you tend to frame your position from your own perspective. You frame the situation according to your beliefs and values and what makes sense to you. This may not, however, make sense, or appeal to the person you are trying to influence. So as an effective communicator, instead of just repeating your perspective, you need to try to give your position a different perspective, more in tune with the others' perspective, so that it is more meaningful to them and therefore you are more likely to be influential.

First, you need to try and understand the other's perspective on the issue and then reframe when you have some information. You need to find out enough about how others view the situation or context, so you know what kind of reframe will fit. You need to ask 'Will this frame have any influence on the other person?' if the answer is no, then you need to look for a different reframe.

It's always best to know something and get information before reframing a position or situation, but if you don't you can hypothesise on the others' likely perspective. You can try to put yourself in their shoes, imagine what the situation is from their perspective, what their concerns are. However, this is much less effective than actually engaging with them to find out their views.

FOR INSTANCE

Let's take a situation where someone in your organisation wants to influence their boss to pay for some training. From their own perspective they will, in all probability, talk about their own development needs and how they haven't had any training for ages. They might even start pointing out that certain other people have been getting a whole lot of training and development over the last few years. By this time they are probably becoming emotional and angry and feeling undervalued compared to these other people! So they are looking at the situation purely from their own perspective.

Now this approach may or may not be effective with their boss, but we think that it's highly unlikely to be an effective approach.

We would suggest that you reframe the person's position, and help them move away from the purely personal perspective used, to one that reframes it to the organisation's perspective. You could then talk about the effect on your colleague and staff if you are poorly trained or lack some specific skills, the effect on the reputation of the organisation if the managers are not up to date with the latest techniques. You can add to the reframe by pointing out, for example, that the training will enable you to share your new skills with your colleagues and staff! So you would be framing the request from the manager's and the organisation's position. You may not be successful but it is much more likely to be influential than just going on about your own needs!

Reframing for yourself

Reframing can be used not just to influence others, but also to convince yourself. If for example, you get feedback that you are obsessive about details, you could become demotivated and depressed. On the other hand you could reframe that as 'I am a bit of a perfectionist!' Of course, most of you will do this automatically in a situation like a job interview. But there is a limit to this type of reframe. If you reframe everything into a positive you may well end up being viewed as unrealistic.

On the other hand many people do tend to frame themselves very negatively, and talk themselves down all the time. This then affects their confidence. So it might be useful to do some reframing in order to increase your confidence. For example, if you frame yourself as 'really unstructured', you are in fact missing out on the positives of your way of working; such as the adaptability, creativity and responsiveness. So you could reframe it as 'I am able to be flexible and work well in chaotic situations.'

One of the clearest examples of reframing was given by American inventor Thomas Edison talking about his attempt to create electric light. He said:

> Every wrong attempt is another step forward. I have not failed 10,000 times. I have successfully found 10,000 ways that will not work!

We are not saying that you should never be critical of yourself, but in terms of influencing others, using the reframing technique can lead to much more positive outcomes.

Using reframing can lead to much more positive outcomes

If you think that someone is pig-headed and then go on to say it to them out loud, the result is likely to be anger, or at best defensiveness. Then you will have difficulty in maintaining an effective working relationship with them. If, however, you reframe this more positively, for example, as tenacity, the outcome is likely to be more positive. If you then continue to reframe it and come up with the frame of 'this person is strong minded and persistent', you are avoiding judgemental language, and leaving the door open to some positive interpretations of strong mindedness. This means that you will be able to see situations where this person's strong mindedness could be used in a positive and useful way. You could then go on to discuss the implications of that strong mindedness without awakening defensive routines.

To reframe like this, you need to ask yourself if there is ever any kind of context in which the person's behaviour would have a positive value. And of course you can use this reframing technique on yourself! So rather than being immediately self-critical about something you see as a weakness, try to figure out where that trait or behaviour could be useful.

So what situations are you in that you can reframe? How do you see your job? Do you regard it as boring and mundane? Try reframing it. Look at it from other people's perspective. This is a trick we use every time we get fed up with our jobs. We look at the people around us who are doing difficult or dangerous jobs and look at our job through their eyes. That usually does the trick and stops us moaning within a minute or two!

Organisational reframing

Organisations use reframing all the time. To take an example, in 2009 Scandinavian Airline company SAS reduced costs, cut down on destinations, saved money and downsized. Normally this is seen as a negative thing and might lead customers to abandon the airline and use other airlines. SAS were clearly conscious of this so they reframed the negative situation into a more positive one. They reframed, re-labelled and communicated the downsizing as 'Core SAS'. **Core** sounds like a fairly positive word. It suggests focusing on the important issues. SAS even talked about 'a new stronger SAS'. The airline have made people redundant, and reduced the number of routes they fly. Yet they are framing this as a positive thing which will give customers 'an even more customer oriented and efficient SAS'. They will get rid of their stakes in other airlines such as Air Baltic, Spanair, Estonia Air, BMI and Skyways. This will be reframed as 'a focus on Nordic air travel market'.

The football club Manchester United does something similar. It wants the club to be known worldwide. This has the advantage of increasing interest worldwide and therefore attracting both fans and sponsors internationally. The club does this very effectively, they have a club shop in Shanghai for example and lots of fans in Thailand, China and the Middle East. Most of these fans have never been to Manchester. The club's ground in Manchester is in the Trafford area of the city and is called Old Trafford. This clearly has meaning for the people who live in Manchester and support the club, but perhaps doesn't have much meaning for the fans in China for example. So Manchester United have reframed their ground, and it is now commonly known as the 'Theatre of Dreams'.

Reframing to develop others

Reframing is a common technique used when coaching and developing others. As an effective leader you too can use it to help develop your people to shift their perspectives and turn them to more positive and useful means.

FOR INSTANCE

One of our coaching clients, John, told Mike about a loss of confidence he had suffered during his career. This was clearly traumatic and had had a fairly serious and negative effect on him. During coaching sessions reframing was used to encourage John to see the loss of confidence (viewed by John as negative) as something more helpful and positive. Without denying the reality of the situation, the coach helped John to reframe it as a transition or turning point, which enabled John to have deeper self-awareness and learning. Reflecting on this John agreed that this period had indeed enabled him to reflect deeply on his core values and he had learned a lot about himself. Reframing the situation for John helped him to see that particular period as much more positive and enabling than he had been able to before the reframe.

The above example illustrates how this technique can be used to good effect to bring about a change of perspective which led to a more positive outcome.

IN SUMMARY ...

To develop your skills to reframe you should:

- Regard reframing as an essential part of your toolkit and practise it regularly.

- Reframe experiences more positively for yourself.

- Develop others by helping them reframe situations so they better understand the positive elements.

- Recognise that all influencing involves reframing. So, beware of other people's perspectives and actively seek to reframe to match others' needs for positive outcomes.

The language of influence and relationship

anguage is one of the key skills used by leaders. In fact, language is the main instrument of influence and persuasion. Although we know that body language and paralinguistics are also hugely important, it doesn't mean that we can just use these to influence. We saw in an earlier section of the book that body language was very important. But we also know that the percentage of communication attributed to body language – 55 per cent in one study – only refers to social situations when emotions are involved. So, if you are speaking on a very factual or logical subject at work then words will take on a much greater significance because as you remove the emotional aspect the words themselves carry more weight.

Types of Language

We have categorised language into six main types which are used in business life.

These are:

▌ powerful language

▌ soft language

▌ creative language

▌ logical language

▌ empathetic language

▌ negative language

Powerful language

This is language that is firm and confident. There are no hesitations. It is direct, straightforward and action oriented. It is positive oriented rather than negative, and so will say 'I will 'rather than '*I'll try*' for example. It means being specific rather than vague. 'I need that report on my desk by end of play Wednesday' rather than 'Do you think you can finish the report as soon as possible'. It is the type of language that managers and leaders will have to be able to use. Though not all of the time! You will need to practise being clear and confident in your language. A word of warning though, we do not mean being arrogant and over assertive, that is a complete turn off.

Soft language

This is language which is hesitant, tentative, question based. It's when you use phrases like 'I wonder'. So for example instead of saying 'Can you help me ', you say, 'I wonder if you could help me?' Or introduce words like *perhaps,* or use '*I'm* sorry' as in 'I'm sorry to disturb you, but…'

Using soft language is often viewed as weak and non-influential, but in certain circumstances it is the right language to use. This is especially true when you want to be, or need to be, seen as being polite. So, for example, in a situation where you have absolutely no power or authority, then the use of soft language would be advisable.

> **FOR INSTANCE**
>
> Maribel Albisua, a manager for a French multi-national company in Mexico told us that how you ask people to do a task is key. She sometimes has to ask her peers over whom she has no formal power, to do things. If she just tells them to do something they will feel she is just bossing them around. So, Maribel uses suggestions rather than commands, and makes sure that she supports and involves her peers, by asking them what they think and if they also have suggestions. This, she says, softens the impact, and makes them feel much more included.

Some people, however, use this type of language too often, and then can be seen as weak and ineffective. The idea is that you should use this type of language flexibly and appropriately. For example, an inappropriate use of soft language would be when you are trying to influence people to join up for something like a book club or wine club. You wouldn't say 'our wines are usually quite good' or 'it might be quite useful to join'.

Creative language

This is language that is sticky, memorable and makes a lasting impression. It tries to be different and creative. It uses symbols, images, metaphors and rhythm. Alliteration is used, strong visual images are created. The user creates stories which resonate with the listener. Novelists, playwrights and poets are the masters of this genre, but as managers we also need to make lasting impressions and engage others. So it's worthwhile thinking about how to use language more creatively. For good examples of this, read some of John Simmons's books.

American advertising guru the late Bill Bernbach created many notable advertising campaigns, including the famous AVIS Rent A Car slogan 'We try harder'. He said 'The truth isn't the truth until people believe you, and they can't believe you if they don't know what you're saying, and they can't know what you're saying if they don't listen to you, and they won't listen to you if you're not interesting, and you won't be interesting unless you say things imaginatively, originally, freshly.'

So don't be afraid to try saying things creatively and differently.

Logical language

This is the language of logic and analysis, of facts and figures, of detail, proofs, structure and graphs. It is clear, analytical, formal and unemotional. It is a common language among leaders and managers and is especially favoured by IT, engineers, accountants and specialists.

Logical language is clearly a useful and necessary one in business. However, facts alone are not sufficient to convince everyone, nor do facts always create effective relations. The major drawback here is not so much the logic itself as the accompanying lack of emotion. This leads to people who use this language not taking other people's feelings and emotions into account.

Facts alone are not sufficient to convince everyone

Empathetic language

This is the language of warmth and empathy. It uses words like feelings and caring. It is question based rather than directive. It is supportive and encouraging. It sympathises with others and shows concern.

Clearly, if you want to engage more effectively with people and develop your relationships at work, you will need to start learning this language. There is some research that suggests that men are not as effective at this as women. So if you are a male manager, and you are in a male dominated sector/industry, and you have a preference for strong and logical language, you will need to be very aware of any shortcomings in using empathetic language. On the other hand, if you consistently use empathetic language, there may be times when this is counterproductive. There may be situations where you should try to use stronger and more direct language, for example, in a male dominated environment.

There is one final type of language we hear people using in business and that is **negative language.** This is a counterproductive way of using language and one that successful leaders will avoid.

Negative language

This is language where you use, for example, wouldn't, shouldn't, couldn't, and mustn't. It is the language where you are constantly nay saying, blaming others and disagreeing, and never actually proposing solutions or positive ideas. The effect of this language on others is demoralising and demotivating and leads to people avoiding you because you sap them of energy.

Other considerations

Choice of language

Generally speaking the first rule is to adapt your language to the culture and situation you find yourself in. If the language used is formal, then you adapt and make your language more formal. If you speak formally and the context is informal, then adapt and modify your language so it sounds less formal. We don't mean you should try and imitate other people's accents though. It is the same with words; listen to the type of words being used. Are people talking about success, winning, action, achieving? Then use similar types of words. If you are working in a competitive environment where these words are common, and then go into a much less competitive environment and start talking about winning and beating your competitors (all things we have heard!) then you are not going to be an effective influencer or create good relationships with your new colleagues.

Language to avoid

Effective leaders and managers take care to avoid using language which could be seen as insulting or counterproductive. Cursing, swearing and aggression can all be seen in this way. It is also important to avoid jargon, acronyms, irritators and phrases such as; 'sort of', 'kind of', 'you know', 'yes but' and 'I know what you are trying to say'. Many people have become quite casual in their use of language and forget about the impact it can have on others. For example: it is common practice today for people to curse and swear in everyday speech. This can be deeply insulting for some people and can therefore have a negative impact on their impression of you and consequently your ability as a leader or manager.

Articulation and pronunciation

You must be careful to articulate properly, as you cannot be influential if others don't understand you. People who are considered to be articulate are often perceived to be powerful and influential.

> You cannot be influential if others don't understand you

Good pronunciation and articulation are especially important in an international environment. We often get comments from international managers like 'You are Scottish, but how come I understand you, but not my Scottish colleague? ' Well it's because while we have kept our Scottish accents we make sure to enunciate clearly at an appropriate pace, and try not to use too many Scottish idioms and phrases. We often meet managers with lovely regional accents, but who do themselves a disservice by speaking far too quickly, not pronouncing clearly and by using too many local words and phrases.

Having a regional accent can also be very positive. Research shows that people from Scotland, Ireland and the north of England are seen to be more friendly and approachable than those from the south of England. However, on the negative side the same research tells us that people from Birmingham and Liverpool are seen as untrustworthy and are viewed as less intelligent. Clearly they are not, but what matters is the perception that they might be. The trick is to keep your accent authentic, yet be flexible enough to modify it so that it is understood.

Irritators

There are a number of words and phrases that are considered to be irritators. Probably the most common one is starting a phrase with the words, 'With all due respect', You just know that when a person says that they are immediately going to follow it with something fairly disrespectful! Of course it can be used deliberately, you can say 'with respect' to clearly indicate that you don't respect the person all that much. A very good example of this was on the BBC Radio 4 programme 'Today' when Lord Mandelson, a former UK Government Minister, was being interviewed by Evan Davis. Davis had been giving the Minister a fairly tough grilling, asking lots of questions and not giving him much time to reply. Mandelson clearly wanted some time to give his point of view, and could easily have let irritation and frustration creep into his voice. To his credit he kept his tone pleasant and interrupted Davis with the words 'Evan, with the greatest love and respect ...!' From then on Davis seemed to drop his dogged grilling, and allow Mandelson much more time. Mandelson, as an experienced politician and, some might say, master of spin, knew that just to say 'with respect' or 'with the greatest respect' would not be influential. But to add 'with the greatest love' is creative, different and disarming.

Grammar

You may not have liked studying grammar at school, but it can be important to speak with the correct grammar. Many of us do not really understand the intricacies of grammar and so often make mistakes. Is it important? Well it depends on the impression you want to make. If you make simple mistakes in grammar, or use local and regional variations, you might well be seen as not being very well educated. That could work against you in certain contexts. For example if you are an ambitious manager, wanting to get promotion, and undertook to network widely in circles like the CBI, Institute of Directors and so on, and you say, for example 'You was', instead of 'You were' it is highly likely that it will reduce your influence and effectiveness. If you are speaking and it is not your first language others are more likely to make allowances.

Adapting your language to the situation and people

'Eloquence is the power to translate a truth into language perfectly intelligible to the person to whom you speak'

Ralph Waldo Emerson. American writer and poet

In many influencing environments you are speaking with
people from either different parts of the UK, or from other
countries. You need to use language that the people you
are talking to can readily understand. This is especially
important when influencing in an international context.
So you need to read the situation you are in, listen to how
people speak, and make allowances. You need to be able
to adapt to a certain degree. For example, we are both
from Scotland, and the Scots have strong regional accents,
use local dialect and also tend to speak very quickly. We
have learned that when working outside Scotland we slow
down, pronounce more clearly and avoid using local dialect
and words. Furthermore, it is important to recognise that
different organisations will have different language protocols
which should be recognised and adapted to.

Processing ideas

There are three major ways people take ideas on board:

▌ Visual

▌ Auditory

▌ Kinaesthetic.

If you are someone who is predominantly Visual your
reference will be sight and you will tend to use words and
phrases like 'let me picture this', ' I see what you mean'. But
if your are predominantly Auditory your reference will be
sound and you will use words and phrases like, 'I hear you',
or 'Sounds like an excellent idea', or 'Got you loud and clear.'
If you are Kinaesthetic your reference will be touch and you
will use words like, 'This doesn't feel right.' Or 'Let's touch
base on this one later.' An example of this is Volkswagen's
current television commercial in the UK for their Golf model
which focusses on the Auditory. It's about the sound the car
door makes when it shuts. They are appealing to our auditory

channel and it makes the advertisement just that bit more creative and memorable. You might find yourself listening to the sound your car door makes when it shuts. Is it a cheap tinny sound or a strong clunky sound like the VW? So listen to the language other people use, and try to fit in to their way of taking things on board and respond accordingly. This will help create rapport and also be more influential.

IN SUMMARY ...

- Think carefully about what you say.
- *How* you say things is critical.
- Listen carefully to how others speak and what kind of language they use.
- Adapt and flex your language to fit the context.
- Think about the type of language you tend to favour.
- Ask friends to give honest feedback about your voice and language.
- Record yourself, listen to it and then plan how you can be more effective.

The art of storytelling

Storytelling is a powerful technique for leaders, it adds to your repertoire for relationship creation, building and development. It can also be an effective aspect of influencing as it is an extremely powerful way of helping you to connect emotionally with others. And, as influencing expert Andrej Huczynski of Glasgow University puts it, 'Emotion expands and seizes the imagination.'

You all have the ability to tell stories which connect to others. Stories have always been with us; you may call them parables, fairytales, legends, myths or fables. But they have affected all of us since our youngest years. Storytelling is not just for kids. It can also be beneficial in organisational and business life.

> You all have the ability to tell stories
> which connect to others

Why is storytelling important?

When told effectively, stories tend to stick in our minds and remain memorable. We bet most of you can remember some of the stories you heard during your childhood from parents or grandparents. Perhaps you remember the stories or funny tales about your family that have been passed down through the generations. These stories are memorable to you and often will often be embellished by you in later years when you use them with your own children. Storytelling in this context is an active process and is no different to the way you can develop stories in relation to your work life.

As a leader, it is important to give some thought to the stories that have affected you during your work life. When you are introducing someone to your organisation, building a relationship, making a presentation or influencing someone about change, stories will often be a major element of the process. In fact, if you think about it, storytelling is a major feature of your day-to-day life.

As an individual you will in all probability use stories when you:

▌ meet someone for the first time and you tell the other person a little about yourself; a brief story about your history;

▌ are inducting a new member of staff, you will no doubt tell them organisational stories to help them understand the culture of the organisation and to help them fit in;

▌ are at job interviews as part of the process of telling others about your prior experience will involve story telling;

▌ socialise or gossip with others when you create and tell stories about your experience or situation;

▌ make a presentation to a group you use stories to add interest, provide examples and make a point;

▌ influence others about a change you wish to bring about; you will no doubt tell stories about the current situation and the future you envisage.

Before we go on to examine some stories and the way they help people and organisations connect emotionally, we would like to introduce the concept of fungibility which will help you to understand the relevance of stories to influence and relationships. Fungibility is a word used to describe products which are interchangeable. So if your product, service or personal skills are similar to others, then one way to differentiate is to tell a good story which illustrates uniqueness.

FOR INSTANCE

Think about when you buy potatoes. Generally speaking we do not buy branded potatoes. We want potatoes to make chips, mashed or roasted potatoes so we don't really care what brand of potatoes we buy. This is fine for us as consumers, but presents a real danger for potato producers.

It means that as consumers we do not differentiate between types of potatoes and therefore are not prepared for the price differentials. If we do not differentiate, we do not care what type of potato we purchase. We will buy it on price and availability, so we can choose the cheapest potato! And if we choose the cheapest potato it leads to lower margins and less profit.

Nowadays there is an attempt by some potato producers to differentiate their product, to give their potato a story! In other words, to de-fungibilise their product! A good example of this would be potatoes from the small island of Noirmoutier in France – the Rolls Royce of potatoes. Now you may not know this, but Noirmoutier is home to the most expensive potatoes in the world. They are called 'La Bonnotte' and only 60 to 100 tons are harvested each year, by hand. They are fertilised by seaweed, command very high prices, have a very good reputation and are prized for their unique flavour. To add to the mystique, the entire production is sold on one day – the first Friday in May. Try Googling the most expensive foods in the world, and you will see these potatoes on the list, alongside Caviar, white truffles and Wagyu beef from Japan. These are clearly not fungible potatoes!

Interestingly, the Potato Pro website (yes there is one!) asks its readers to reflect on how they can think out of the box and find opportunities there might be for other special potatoes. This is a call in effect to 'Bonnottise' other producers' more mundane potatoes!

Personal and Interpersonal stories

Creating a personal story will help you to create an emotional connection with others and to differentiate yourself. Stories are not the only way to build connections, but they are a useful, effective and creative way of doing so. Facts are important, but the key lesson is that they are never going to be enough for really effective relationship building and influencing. People usually want more than just the facts. They want informal information to back up the facts. They are interested to hear your story, and when they ask you about your story they don't want to hear just a chronological explanation of your career. It is much better to weave it into a story about your career so far! You are more than a collection of facts, so, think about what is important to you, talk about you and your family, and tell them about your heritage, your values and your passions. Always make them relevant to the topic, people and situation you are currently in. Explain what is unique and different about you and your ideas. That way you will have greater impact and people will remember you and your story.

Think about what is important to you

FOR INSTANCE

David believes that changing his approach to illustrating his background during a recent job interview was significant in his success. In previous job interviews he had adopted a typically chronological approach to discussing his education and job history. On this occasion he decided to take a storytelling approach and used the metaphor of a journey to share his background with the interviewers.

Rather than talk about key dates and job roles he told the story about his values, beliefs, vision, key decisions and achievements along the route. He sensed that the interviewers were far more engaged with this approach than the more traditional chronological way. Their feedback to him when he accepted the job was that he stood out from the other interviewees as being better prepared, memorable and more compelling. Of course, David also had relevant qualifications and experience for the role.

For example, an exercise we do with our MBA students is to sit them all in a circle, and ask them to tell us their full name and to explain the story behind the name. On the face of it this seems simple, and you might be asking yourself what the point is. The point is that it allows each student to tell us their own unique story, which involves why they were given their first and middle names and also the story behind their surnames. It's especially powerful in an international group and generates huge interest and emotion. Why is it so powerful? Because no one has ever asked them the story behind their name before – they had never had the opportunity of speaking in public about it. And of course behind every name there is a fascinating story. Try it. Ask your colleagues the story behind their names. You will undoubtedly learn something more about them and their family, and it will help you to connect and to deepen your relationship with them.

One of the proofs that we as humans love stories is the prevalence of rumours and gossip in our organisations. We hear things on the grapevine, repeat them, embellish them so that when they get back to the people concerned the story has taken on vast new dimensions that can be very far removed from the truth. We are all likely to have been the victim of rumour or gossip at some point in our careers. But the fact is that if you don't tell your story, many people are quite happy to make up a story about you and tell others that story.

Another aspect of storytelling is framing it in an appropriate way. On occasions people have unhelpful experiences which they translate into a negative story about themselves. This can lead to loss of confidence and self-esteem. In situations like this it can be helpful to reframe the story (see Chapter 18) in a more positive and useful way.

Organisational stories

Organisations use stories to:

▌ create and develop their image in the marketplace

▌ build their brand. As marketing expert and author Tony Cram says '*The essence of a good brand is a good story*'

▌ make their advertising campaigns more memorable.

FOR INSTANCE

The UK bread brand 'Hovis' has created an excellent story accompanied by a series of television commercials telling us that Hovis is the same loaf now as it's always been.

If you Google Hovis on the internet you will find the tag line 'Hovis – As Good As It's Always Been' in pride of place on their website, where they tell of their 120-year history. They have developed a story based on their history of tradition, quality and nostalgia around their bread in order to distinguish it from the hundreds of other varieties of bread on the market today. They have even produced a book telling the story of Hovis throughout these 120 years.

Using storytelling in business life is all about making something memorable to create differentiation and also begin an emotional connection with others.

Many of the best known international companies are excellent at telling a compelling story. UK-based soft drinks company Innocent is a good example of a company deliberately telling a story and creating a narrative to go with it. The result is that they have a more emotional connection with their customers. As well as having a clear and compelling story they also have clear values connected to the story.

FOR INSTANCE

The Innocent Story – Innocent was founded by three Cambridge graduates – Richard Reed, Adam Balon and Jon Wright in 1999. The three were friends at university and before founding Innocent, had previously worked in consulting and advertising. The story of their company tells us that in 1998 they decided to sell their smoothie fruit drinks from a stall at a music festival in London. People were asked to put their empty cups in a 'yes' or 'no' bin depending on whether they thought Richard, Adam and Jon should quit their jobs and start making the fruit drinks full time. At the end of the festival, the story tells us, the 'YES' bin was full, with only three cups in the 'NO' bin. They resigned from their jobs the following day.

The Innocent Company has created a memorable story which writer John Simmons describes as creating a legend! This legend, along with excellent products and strong values (make money ethically, create healthy products, and donate at least 10 per cent of profits to charity) has given them considerable commercial success. For example, they were number 40 in the *Sunday Times* fast Track 100 list in 2007 and had doubled their turnover year on year. Their narrative involves the founding story, or myth, plus their quirky advertising, the catchy name and their open communication style. They invite anyone who wants to chat to call them on their 'banana' phone and to pop in to see them at their headquarters, the aptly named 'Fruit Towers'.

One of the dangers they may face, however, is that in 2009 Coca Cola acquired a stake in the company. It remains to be seen how they can continue to live their story and their values. The 'Innocent' story of three college friends founding the company on the basis of festival goers liking their smoothies, and strong ethical values, may not stand up as well when a multinational like Coca Cola is involved.

Storytelling, relationship building and influence

As we have seen, storytelling affects relationship building and influencing at two levels. The first level is at the interpersonal level, and the second one is at the company or organisational level. At the interpersonal level, we need to be able to relate and connect emotionally through the use of stories, metaphors and analogies. Stories not only deepen the emotional connection, they are also sticky – that is to say, memorable!

At the organisational level, companies and organisations use storytelling to connect with us and to try to influence us every day. So we need better to understand this process so that we can create stories at the organisation level in order to better influence both our internal and external customers.

Here at Ashridge we have a history going back some 700 years. A history of monks and learning, of holy relics brought back from the Crusades, of Kings and Queens such as King Henry VIII and Queen Elizabeth I (the Virgin Queen).

A history of entrepreneurs like the Duke of Bridgewater, known as the Canal Duke, who created the first canals in England, and innovative landscape gardeners like Capability Brown and Humphry Repton. In other words a very good story!

When we tell our students and participants that King Henry VIII used to love coming here to hunt, or that the monks in the 1200s used to have a library – some of whose books still exist, or that we used to have (or maybe still have) a phial of Holy Blood brought here by the Holy Roman Emperor, or that Queen Elizabeth I used to live here, or that one of the greatest English entrepreneurs, the Canal Duke, lived here, it makes a difference to them. They are now part of the Ashridge story, a story that involves learning, leadership and entrepreneurship going back more than 700 years!

So what is your organisation's story? How does your organisation connect emotionally to its clients and its employees for that matter?

What is your organisation's story?

What is your personal story? What are you communicating? And if you think that you're not trying to communicate anything, think again! Others are aware of you, and are making assumptions about you. So if you're not telling them your story they're definitely creating a story when they see and hear you. If you don't tell them your story, they will invent one for you anyway, and it won't be as positive or as accurate as your own one. Our colleague, Tony Cram says, 'If you do not tell them a story they're making it up for themselves!' The implications for your influencing and your relationships are clear. What stories are you telling about yourself, your department, your product, your service, your company? Compelling stories lead to compelling influence.

Good stories paint a picture of a desired state or future. They tell you about the roots of the company or product, its background, where it is coming from. These stories differentiate the companies from their competitors. Good stories differentiate more than poor stories, or than no stories. Stories can range from multi-million pound brand campaigns through to low cost word of mouth stories.

The message is clear – don't allow yourself or your company to become a commodity. Get yourself a story! Look back at the origins of the company for example, or at the values of the founders, or any key present day values. Tell us what you do differently or better. Remember that stories can be explicit or implicit. If you create an explicit story, make sure it is connected to reality. The reality has to match up to the story. If it doesn't, if the story is just a story with no link to reality, you will lose influence, relationships, credibility and customers.

Implicit stories are the ones that customers tell about you. They can be positive or negative. If they are negative make sure you hear about them and do something about it. Don't hide bad stories away and pretend they don't exist. Bad stories grow faster than good ones. If the stories are positive, then the same thing applies. Build on these stories and make people aware of them both internally and externally.

Don't hide bad stories away

Another excellent example of storytelling is the branding of a renovated garden in Cornwall. Tim Smit, is the co-founder of the famous Eden project in Cornwall, the largest greenhouse in the world. Before creating the Eden Project, he had undertaken with others to renovate an old abandoned garden at Heligan in Cornwall that he and Tim Willis (a descendant of the Tremayne family – hereditary owners of the house and gardens) had discovered. In an interview with Peter Cook, author of *Rock and Roll Leadership*, Smit explained how he had learned a lot from the music business, and that no one had ever had the idea of marketing a garden before. What he wanted to do was make the restoration project like an album sleeve, something that people would possess in their memory. So he came up with the idea of calling the garden '**The Lost Gardens of Heligan**'. He also realised that he needed a narrative to graft on to the name, so he described the garden as a stage where people had led their lives unchanging for hundreds of years. Smit realised that as people came to see the gardens they were seeing them through his story.

Now we have no particular interest in gardens, but as soon as we heard the name – the Lost Gardens of Heligan, we wanted to go and see them. We found the name intriguing and evocative. It conjured up images from childhood, ideas of lost treasure and pirates. It motivated us to make the long trip from London down to Cornwall to see them. We're not sure that we would have made the effort if they had simply been called 'The renovated garden' or 'An old garden which we have renovated' or 'Tremayne Gardens'.

Tim Smit has continued this story and theme by writing a book about the gardens and by describing the different areas of the gardens in ways that are consistent with his narrative. So if you go there you will explore the Jungle and the Lost Valley, stroll down the Butler's path, visit the Sundial Garden and the Pencolenick Glasshouse, walk along the Georgian Ride and ramble through the Ravine Rockery! So, has the Heligan story worked? Well, it has won a string of awards, been voted the nation's favourite garden in 2002, came 2nd only to the world famous Kew gardens as the nation's finest garden in 2003 and it attracts more than 210,000 visitors every year.

Of course the gardens would have been just as beautiful without the story, but we doubt that they would have been as popular and successful without the great narrative.

The future for influencing others lies in making a distinction between your product/service and those of the competition. One of the key ways of doing this is to tell (or on a more cynical note) invent, a good story.

IN SUMMARY …

It is worth considering your stories about:

- You the individual
    - what do you stand for?
    - what are your values and beliefs?
- Your work group
- Your organisation.

Telling a good story, rather than just giving plain facts is one of the most effective ways to differentiate you, your brand or your organisation from your competitors. Stories engage the heart and the emotions and are much more memorable, stickier if you like, than a list of facts and figures. Stories give context and meaning, emotion and impact.

As the late Bill Bernbach, American advertising guru, said 'Logic and analysis can immobilise and sterilise an idea. It's like love, the more you analyse it, the faster it disappears.'

Your approach to influence

nfluencing is a key element for engaging and relating to others. Your influence approach is the one you typically use when you are trying to persuade others. Let's call it your natural way of trying to get things done in the way you want them done. We all tend to have a preference in terms of the approach we adopt, and so we use that approach regularly and tend to feel very comfortable with it. We may not even be aware that we are using a particular approach until other people point it out to us. This approach might well be effective, but because we often use it automatically, without reflecting on it, it may not in fact be the best one to use in a particular environment or context.

Sticking to your normal approach can have a number of drawbacks:

▌ you might be using the wrong approach for the specific people involved in the issue

▌ you risk alienating people as they will not always respond to your approach

▌ you may be seen as inflexible and not adapting to the situation or context.

The appropriate choice of influencing approach, and the skill with which you use it, will have a strong impact on the outcome and success of your influencing. So rather than just using your normal influencing approach, we are suggesting that you reflect on the people you need to influence, and that you think about the context and environment you are influencing in. Then decide on the most appropriate approach for the situation.

Reflect on the people you need to influence

By adopting the appropriate approach at the beginning of an influencing discussion you will significantly increase the chances of having a positive effect upon the influencing process and on the final outcome. Our work with managers shows us they use four main influencing approaches.

The four influencing approaches

The four approaches are:

- **Assertive** – you influence in a straightforward and candid way, expressing what you want and the way you want it done

- **Rational** – you influence by presenting your case using reasoning and evidence

- **Participative** – you influence by involving and engaging interpersonally with others

- **Inspirational** – you influence by arousing enthusiasm and passion and engaging others' emotions.

Each of the approaches has its own characteristics, advantages and disadvantages. One approach is not 'better' than another, rather they are different. What is important is that you are able to choose the appropriate approach (or

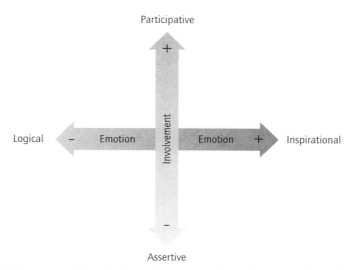

Figure 21.1 The 4 influencing approaches (© Brent and Beech)

combination of approaches) for the people, the context, and the specific influencing issue you are facing, and that you are able to use them skilfully. The problem is that most of us fall into the trap of relying on a single approach. This is usually the one you are used to, the one you use confidently and which seems comfortable to you. Consequently you will not be using the full range of approaches and therefore may be missing opportunities to influence most effectively.

Below are some of the details and characteristics of the four approaches.

Assertive Approach

There is an authoritative aspect in this approach which has three different elements. One is personal authority, the authority and confidence that comes naturally to some people. Another is the authority that comes with experience and expertise, and the third is the authoritative presence that comes from confidence in your job position and the decision making role that goes with this.

It is important to differentiate this third element, job position, from pure reliance on job status, as a basis for commanding obedience from others. Getting obedience on the basis of your formal authority and job position alone is not an effective influence approach. Having confidence in your job position and having the confidence to make decisions is an assertive approach, but is different to power based use of authority. If you rely exclusively on your formal authority to get things done, then you cannot be said to be influencing others. You are ordering them what to do, and in the long run, you will end up alienating people. There is nothing wrong in using the assertive approach if it is done skilfully and appropriately.

Characteristics of approach

If you use this approach you are likely to be energetic, action oriented and challenging. In debates you are willing to take people on and stick your head above the parapet. You are likely to communicate in an articulate manner, showing confidence in your voice and body language. You adopt an assertive, direct and confident way of influencing. You are clear about where you want to go and what you want to happen. This approach involves more advocacy than inquiry, more telling than asking.

When to use it

The approach works when as well as your formal power you also have the respect of others. This means that you will be listened to because of that respect and relationship and not solely because of your formal hierarchical position. You would be likely also to adopt this approach when people's health, safety and security are at risk.

It could also prove to be effective when influencing people who lack self-confidence, or you are working with a group of relatively new or inexperienced people, who have little or no knowledge of the organisation. The downside is that although using the assertive approach will be effective in the short term, you will not be building their confidence in the long run. The skill here is to know when to use the assertive approach and when to start incorporating the other approaches in order to appeal to and involve others. The real skill is to know when to adjust your approach as people become more experienced. If you remain wedded to the assertive approach it will become less effective and could even be counterproductive.

The real skill is to know when to adjust your approach

It can also be used effectively where it fits in with the organisational and national culture. For example, it would work in high power distance cultures, such as China, India, Kazakhstan and Uzbekistan where they have structured and hierarchical cultures. Additionally, it will be effective in organisational cultures where a formal, top-down approach is the norm.

The assertive approach will tend to be counterproductive when used with people who are skilled and knowledgeable about the issue being discussed. Especially if you have not established your own expertise or track record and don't have an effective relationship with them. They will feel that you are pushing things through, and not using their knowledge and experience.

If you choose this approach regularly you should be aware that you are likely to be regarded as ignoring others' perspectives, and that you may be perceived as closed minded and arrogant and this could ultimately lead to trust and respect issues in your work relationships.

Many people do however, find this approach appealing, because it can be simple and direct and allows people to understand their role and what's expected of them. But its overuse can breed passivity in your people.

FOR INSTANCE

In one team event that Mike facilitated in an international pharmaceutical company, one of the team members was a Nobel prize winner. He used his experience, expertise and credibility during the debates and needless to say the others (although experts themselves) tended to listen!

This was an effective use of the assertive approach. He had been invited because of his specific knowledge and experience, and it was appropriate and relevant for him to share it in this context.

Had the event been more of a brainstorming event then this approach would have been inappropriate as it could have intimidated others and prevented them from contributing fully.

You might use this approach when you have expert knowledge of a subject, or if you have been successful in a particular area and you want to get your opinion over in a clear and direct way.

There are, of course, many advantages if you use this approach. You get your point over to others quickly, it doesn't waste a lot of time, and you can be very clear about what you expect to happen. It also has a number of disadvantages: you can appear aggressive and arrogant, you won't be involving the others, therefore you may not be winning them over fully, and you are unlikely to be creating long-term commitment.

The approach can also work when dealing with others of a similar hierarchical level and who probably have knowledge and experience of the area under discussion and who therefore feel comfortable and have the necessary confidence to enter into debate and discussion. They will have the confidence to challenge you, and your assertiveness will be viewed as you having a clear and confident perspective.

At a personal level it is probably also best where, in addition to your strong belief that your suggestions are correct, you also have significant knowledge and experience. Otherwise people will think you are just spouting hot air. Failure to succeed using this approach is usually because of the way you convey your message to others. For example your tone of voice might sound peremptory, or you don't recognise that others have a desire to contribute and you ignore them. You can also fail if you cannot back your case up with sufficient reasons and if you don't convey to others your level of commitment to and belief in the issue.

As we have said people can find this approach appealing, and will often relate to it and buy in to your point of view when you present a persuasive, articulate and convincing case for their support. This is especially true if this is linked to a consistency of your behaviour in relation to the issue.

Rational Approach

This is very much a preferred approach among managers and organisations. It is essentially an approach where you prefer to deal in logic rather than emotion. It is a hard, left brain type of approach, and managers who use it are often suspicious of softer, more emotional and right brained approaches. As the culture of many organisations values rationality, logic and objectivity, this approach is often used to great effect. The potential problem is that it can be overused, ignoring the reality that people are emotional beings as well as rational ones. We know that emotions do play a huge part in decision making, so if you overuse this approach, you will not be as effective as you could be in terms of influencing others successfully.

> Emotions play a huge part in decision making

Characteristics

People who use this approach are often regarded as analytical, logical and objective. They like facts, figures and proofs. People who are successful in using this approach are well prepared, have done their research and established the pros and cons for their case.

They take time to research things, get the facts, and are good with details. Sometimes their rational approach can seem lacking in emotion, and may cause them to be regarded as too cold, impersonal or even arrogant. Rational people believe that because they have spent time researching the issue and looking at the facts, they are going to be right. They have done their homework on the cold facts (as they see it) but they often haven't done enough homework on other people's perspectives and emotions. For example, one manager we met complained that his reason for not being influential was that he was always right but that his team didn't agree with him! We pointed out to him that being right is good, but it's certainly not enough. And that is a trap that the rational people among us fall into, thinking that logic and analysis will be enough to win the argument. It is necessary, but it's rarely enough!

The exclusive use of this approach can lead to a lack of support or commitment from others.

FOR INSTANCE

Jean-Jacques is a Technical Manager in a French multinational company. He is very logical, straightforward, loyal, hardworking and committed, but very black and white in his attitude. He just wants to get on with things and doesn't understand the politics and posturing that go on inside the company. He is successful but he is lacking perhaps in the finer nuances of organisational politics and diplomacy, and as his career progresses he may find that being right is not enough, and that facts and figures are not sufficient to win arguments and gain agreement. He will need to develop his capabilities to be more confident using the other approaches in order to be more effective. Additionally, learning to be more patient, taking time to listen and probe and developing creativity will help Jean-Jacques realise his full potential as a leader. It will also enable him to engage more effectively with others, build relationships and influence successfully.

When to use it

You can effectively use the approach when the issue you are facing is unambiguous and has a clearly identified solution. Not all issues we face are complex and ambiguous, so logic is appropriate here. You can use it when you know there is very definitely a right and a wrong answer to an issue and you can demonstrate why you have the right answer by putting forward a rational well thought through case.

Of course it is also an effective approach when the subject area is highly technical or theoretical and where there are no major emotional issues. Those of you who prefer the rational approach however, often tend to think that there are no emotional issues, or if there are, think that they are irrelevant! We know, however, that people are emotional creatures, are rarely purely logical, and emotional awareness is necessary to be a really effective influencer. Unfortunately logical people do not always have that necessary awareness.

The approach will also be effective when your credibility as an expert is very high. That is when the other people are confident in your expertise. There is a difference between *being* an expert and *being perceived* to be an expert. Too many experts don't take the time to fully establish their credibility, or build a relationship with their audience.

Participative Approach

This is an interdependent style where one of the main aims is to involve others in the process. People who use this approach know that although they might have views and perspectives on an issue, they are not likely to have all the answers. They know that they may need input from others in order to reach the most effective outcome possible. Or, maybe, they think that they do have the right answer, but they are also aware of the fact that allowing their people to get involved is a key aspect of effective leadership.

Characteristics

This approach consists of asking many questions and listening actively to the responses. You ask questions, invite reactions and take the time to consider them. This approach means that you do more inquiring than advocating, more asking than telling. It is about involving people, bringing them into the conversation and working to identify common ground. Its main aim is to find some common ground between positions so that there is a link or bridge between position A and position B. Bridging involves making the distance between two or more positions shorter, therefore making it easier for people to agree.

The participative person is a skilled questioner – using open and probing questions and expanding the others person's initial position.

When to use

You might use this approach when you require long-term commitment and when you are not the expert in a particular subject area, or indeed when there are no obvious solutions to a difficult and complex issue. Many of the issues we now face in organisations are extremely complex and ambiguous, with no one easy answer available. So the only appropriate course of action would be to invite many different perspectives before embarking on a particular course of action.

One advantage of this approach is that it builds on the thoughts and ideas of all the people involved. This will lead to more effective and creative solutions and it is also more likely to gain commitment as you are involving others from the beginning.

There are some potential disadvantages to this approach. If you are in a situation where a quick decision is essential – this approach would not be recommended. The whole basis of the approach is about involving others, so you will need some time. Some managers think all decisions need to be made in a hurry, so if you are that type of manager, stop for a moment and consider the implications of rushing too quickly to a decision. It can also be quite frustrating if you use the participative approach with inexperienced people, or people who lack specific knowledge about the issue or situation. They will wonder why you are involving them, when they are expecting you to tell them what to and how to do it.

FOR INSTANCE

Phil was undertaking a consultancy assignment in Tashkent – the capital of Uzbekistan. Using his preferred influencing approach he adopted a participative stance with the team who were all Uzbek managers and business people. All he got for his efforts to involve them and ask questions was a puzzled silence.

Reflecting later that day on the norms and customs of Uzbek society he realised that he needed to adopt a more directive approach. The Uzbek managers saw Phil as an expert who had come to share his knowledge with them, and they were very surprised and confused when he started asking them about their thoughts and opinions. This example illustrates the need to adopt the appropriate approach to suit the people, situation and environment.

In some contexts this approach might be seen as you not knowing your stuff, as lacking in expertise or being indecisive.

Participative is also very popular with leaders and managers and for many it is their default approach, used as a matter of course without even attempting to use any of the other approaches. It is highly involving and creates a positive climate where all the stakeholders feel they have contributed to the debate. They are therefore committed to and buy into the outcome. However, it will not work well in certain situations or cultures where a hierarchical approach and top-down decision making are the norm.

Inspirational Approach

This is a creative and transformational style. The main aims are to appeal to the emotions of others and to create energy and enthusiasm for change. We all need to be inspired at some time or other and this approach is particularly appropriate when starting major change projects and when you need to capture hearts and minds. The challenge is to both maintain the energy and momentum and to recognise when to bring in the other approaches in order to continue influencing effectively. It is important to recognise that inspiration gets people interested but is never sufficient to bring about long-term change. Managers who use this approach successfully understand when to move onto one of the other approaches.

> We all need to be inspired at some time or other

Characteristics

People who use this approach are highly creative and articulate in presenting themselves. They are confident and eloquent using expressive vocal and body language, and are regarded as visionary and motivational. For example, many famous orators have used this approach to energise and influence their audiences – John Kennedy, Tony Blair, Nelson Mandela, Winston Churchill and Barack Obama to name a few. On a less positive note, this approach is not always used for the common good and can be used by dictators. For example, Adolf Hitler was effective in influencing others and used symbols and other tools to build support for his Nazi policies. Other downsides include the fact that it can appear lacking in detail or be too abstract and vague, especially to logical and national people.

Using this approach usually has a future focus and involves creativity and innovation when presenting your ideas. These include for example, the use of metaphor, storytelling, pictures, diagrams and imagery.

When to use

When you want people to commit to and engage with shared goals, vision or values, it is beneficial to adopt this approach. It is an effective way of getting others' attention, interest and buy in at the start of a new project. What you need to do then is to bring people on board, overcome resistance to change and create lots of energy. Many managers and politicians have discovered that logic is not enough to bring about change, especially if it is complex. In fact, if you are too logical and don't inspire and connect with others emotions, you may fall at the first hurdle. You really need to get beyond pure logic here and start to involve people's emotions and imagination.

Logic is not enough to bring about change

Again it is not the appropriate approach to use when you are facing time constraints or where there are clearly defined procedures or solutions.

FOR INSTANCE

During Obama's US presidential campaign we saw much evidence of the inspirational approach. He appealed to the ordinary person by giving them hope for a better America. He constantly spoke of a better future and a positive vision. His slogan 'yes we can' appealed to the desire for change. Not only was he inspirational but he was also inclusive and participative in his approach.

IN SUMMARY ...

Blindly sticking to one approach and using it as your default influencing approach is rarely effective. It is always best to consider the circumstances, the people and the problem and then select the appropriate approach in order to reach the most effective outcome. Nigel Melville, President and Chief Executive of American Rugby puts it like this,' You have to move up and down the continuum of approaches, the real skill is in judging when to use them, and how.'

You need to be able to judge the correct approach for the situation. Do you need to gain commitment or compliance? If you need commitment then you have to invest time in understanding all the different perspectives and typically participative, inspirational and to some extent rational should be used. If, however, compliance is what you are seeking, the assertive and rational approaches are most appropriate. The problem with compliance however, is that there can be unintended consequences. It can lead to a situation where there will be few challenges, little questioning and no creativity. Ultimately, this leads to lack of engagement, low levels of initiative and poor morale.

As we have said, no one approach is more effective than any other. To be a really effective influencer you need to be able, firstly, to assess a situation, then diagnose the most appropriate approach and develop your skills in all four approaches. This means that you may find yourself using a range of the approaches in any given influencing situation rather than a single approach.

We believe that most of us get 'stuck' using our preferred approach. If you explore different approaches and techniques you can develop the ability to vary your style to suit the situation and people and thus become even more effective. If you only stick to one approach it's a bit like a golfer playing with one club instead of the fourteen in their bag. You might get round the course, but you are never going to be a great golfer!

And finally ...

You will now have a greater understanding of and appreciation for, the importance of relationships at work. This is often cynically referred to as 'the soft stuff' and as you now know this is essential for business success and it is hard!

However, there is a huge difference between understanding the need to do something and actually doing it. As Aristotle said 'We are what we repeatedly do. Excellence then is not an act but a habit.' So the secret to success is to take account of all the tools, tips and techniques and make them a habit.

Here are some final ideas to help you build all of this into your work:

- **Start small** – be specific, identify small achievable changes to work on to get you moving in the right direction.

- **Get help** – look for support from close colleagues, friends and family. Try to find a mentor within your organisation and consider using an external coach from time to time.

- **Notice the changes** – be aware of any differences in your behaviour and approach and notice the reactions of others to these differences. What has changed? Consider the impact this is having on your relationships.

- **Get feedback** – don't just wait for feedback, actively ask others their views on the changes you are trying to make. Remember it's important to listen and understand feedback rather than defending and justifying why you do anything.

- **Practise** – none of this will work unless you try it. You need to try things out, others need to see you doing something differently. It's only a theory unless you actually put it into practice and demonstrate change to others.

- **Reflect and review regularly** – successful leaders and managers take time to review their behaviours and reflect on the impact and consequences.

- **Continue to develop** – dip into this book from time to time to refresh your understanding. Read other books on relevant subjects, consider where you might need further training and get the development you need to be an influential leader.

Good luck in all your working relationships and influencing discussions!

References

Books

Albrecht, K. (2006) *Social Intelligence: The new science of success*. Jossey Bass

Cook, P. (2009) *Sex, Leadership and Rock and Roll: Leadership lessons from the Academy of Rock*. Crown House Publishing

Covey, S. M. R. (2006) *The Speed Of Trust: The one thing that changes everything*. Simon & Schuster

Cram, T. (1994) *The Power of Relationship Marketing*. FT Prentice Hall

Dent, F. E. (2000) *The Leaders Pocketbook*. Management Pocketbooks

Dent, F. E. and Brent, M. (2006) *Influencing, Skills and Techniques For Business Success*. Palgrave

Dent, F. E. (2009) *The Working Relationship Pocketbook*. Management Pocketbooks

Fredrickson, B. (2009) *Positivity*. Crown Publishers

Goffee, R. and Jones, G. (2006) *Why Should Anyone Be Led By YOU? What it takes to be an authentic leader*. HBS Press

Goleman, D. (1996) *Emotional Intelligence: Why it can matter more than IQ*. Bloomsbury Publishing

Huczynski, A. (2004) *Influencing within Organisations*. Routledge

Jensen, R. (1999) *The Dream Society*. McGraw-Hill

Jones, P., Van Hool, J. and Hailstone, P. (2004) *The Impact and Presence Pocketbook*. Management Pocketbooks

Jackson, P. Z. and McKergow, M. (2006) *The Solutions Focus: Making coaching and change simple*. Nicholas Brealey

Kline, N. (1998) *Time to Think*. Cassell Illustrated

Mehrabian, A. (1981) *Silent Messages: Communications of emotions and attitudes*. Wadsworth Publishing Co

Pease, B. and A. (2006) *The Definitive Book of Body Language*. Bantam

Pfeffer, J. (1998) *The Human Equation: Building profits by putting people first*. Harvard Business School Press

Pink, D. (2009) *Drive: The surprising truth about what motivates us*. Riverhead Hardcover

Reis, H. and Sprecher, S. (eds) (2009) Gable S., in *Encyclopaedia of Human Relationships*. Sage

Rogers, Carl (1995) *On Becoming A Person*. Mariner Books

Shea, M. (1994) *Personal Impact: The art of good communication*. Mandarin

Simmons, J. (2006) *The Invisible Grail*. Cyan Books

Smit, T. (2005) *The Lost Gardens of Heligan*. Orion

Sullivan, L. (2003) *Hey Whipple Squeeze This!* J. Wiley & Sons

Interview with Tim Smit by Peter Cook

Journal articles

Fredrickson, B. and Losada, M. (2005) Positive affect and the complex dynamics of human flourishing. *American Psychologist*, 60 (7) 678–86

Losada, M (1999) The Complex Dynamics of High Performance Teams. *Mathematical and Computer Modelling*, 30 (9–10) 179–192

Luft, J. and Ingham, H. (1955) The Johari Window, A Graphic Model of Interpersonal Awareness. *Proceedings of the Western Training Body in Group Development*. LA, UCLA

Luft, Joseph, The Johari Window: A Graphic Model Of Awareness in Interpersonal Relations – *Human Relations Training News* (1961)

Dunbar, R. I. M. (2004) Gossip in Evolutionary Perspective. *Review of General Psychology*. Vol 8 No 2

Websites

Ashridge Website www.ashridge.com
Innocent Website www.innocent.com
SAS Website www.sas.com

Questionnaires

Emotional Competence Inventory (ECI)
Myers Briggs Type Indicator (MBTI)
Strength Deployment Inventory (SDI)

Courses

▌ Creating Working Relationships Programme – A three-day programme run by Ashridge Business School

▌ Influencing Strategies and Skills – A five-day programme run by Ashridge Business School

Index

READ ON

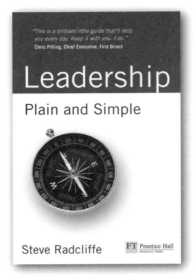

9780273730897

9780273732044

HOW TO
LEAD

2nd Edition

JO OWEN

9780273721505

Simon Cooper

brilliant
Leader

What the best
leaders know,
do and say

9780273720591

Available now online and at all good bookstores

www.pearson-books.com